MILNER CRAFT SERIES

A WRITING ON STONE BOOK

WILD ABOUT WOOL

DESIGNS FOR EMBROIDERERS

LIZ WALSH

SALLY MILNER PUBLISHING
&
WRITING ON STONE

First published in 1997 by
Sally Milner Publishing Pty Ltd
RMB 54 Burra Road
Burra Creek
NSW Australia 2620
in association with
Writing on Stone Pty Ltd
Canberra

© Liz Walsh 1997

Design and typesetting by ANU Graphics, Canberra
Photography by Ben Wrigley
Styling by Sarah Houseman
Illustrations in stitch glossary by Robin Roenfelt
Printed and bound in Hong Kong

Cataloguing-in-Publication data:

    Walsh, Liz, 1943-
    Wild about Wool: designs for embroiderers

    ISBN 1 86351 204 7.

    1. Embroidery. 2. Embroidery – Patterns. I. Title
    (Series: Milner craft series).

    746.44041

Contents

Introduction
2

Materials
3

Working Methods
4–5

Stitch Glossary
6–7

Flower Glossary
8–21

Colour Plates
23–34

Projects

Acknowledgments
95

Suppliers
96

Vest Pattern
97

Thread Conversion Chart
98

Introduction

I grew up on Neptune and Kangaroo Islands, both isolated areas of South Australia. My father was a lighthouse keeper and most of my childhood was spent in out of the way places where my sister and I learnt to amuse ourselves. My mother's philosophy was, 'if it can be made, it can be made at home!' This lead to my learning to sew, knit and do other craft work at an early age.

Living on the islands meant that we spent much time outdoors, which instilled in me a love of nature. I now live in the small town of Strathalbyn in South Australia. It is a beautiful part of the world, an area known for its artists and craftspeople.

Embroidery seemed a natural progression for me from the sewing and craft work that I have always done. I learnt the stitches as a child but the impetus to cover everything with flowers came from the need to cover a damaged spot on an expensive new blouse. I embroidered a design that just seemed to keep growing. Needlework has since become a large part of my life and something of an obsession.

Embroidery is a portable and sociable pastime. I get together with a group of friends once a fortnight to embroider and chat. We learn many things from each other and get lots of work done in spite of the noise! As a member of the Embroiders Guild of South Australia I have spent many happy hours exchanging ideas and learning from others. I love teaching embroidery and get a great lift from watching others becoming enthusiastic about their craft. I see their ideas blossom!

Wool, being a natural fibre, is lovely to work with. It is soft and forgiving, and easy on the hands and eyes. It is also a durable fibre that covers an area quickly. The quickly-forming embroidery is attractive to beginners as they can see the effect in a very short time.

Wool dyes easily—the colours ranging from clear primary reds and bright yellow to the softer more subtle shades of green and grey, so necessary for creating Australian wildflowers.

The natural shades of Kirra wool are perfect for my designs as they capture the spectrum of colours found in the bush. Using these colours really is like 'painting with thread'. The subtle shades vary from the greys and greens of Eucalyptus leaves, to the warm yellows and gold of Banksias and Wattles.

Many of my ideas come from my garden where native shrubs and trees attract blue wrens, parrots and honeyeaters. When I see a particular bird or flower that I would like to use in my designs I use art, botanical and natural history books as a guide. It is easier to translate two-dimensional images into embroidery designs than copying from a photograph. But I have found that it is important to know how flowers are constructed. The number of petals, the shape of the buds and leaves and the different colours. These books show the essential features of the subject in two-dimensional form. This is helpful when I want to exaggerate certain qualities in the embroidery, such as pollen dust on eucalyptus flowers.

This book has been written for anyone with an interest in embroidery and I hope it will encourage those just starting out, and provide inspiration and ideas for experienced embroiderers. Each flower and bird may be used individually, so that you can make up your own designs. The important thing is to have fun. I hope you enjoy the doing and the finished product.

Liz

Materials

FABRICS

I find a natural fibre background fabric works the best for wool embroidery. Natural fibres do not damage the thread. Wool flannel, linen, heavy slub cotton and wool blanketing are excellent choices. I prefer to work on wool flannel because it is heavy enough to support the embroidery. Light fabrics will cause the work to become distorted when the stitches are heavy.

THREADS

There are numerous wool embroidery threads on the market. Most of the work in this book is done in Kirra yarn, two ply weight.

Kirra is 60% mohair and 40% wool. It comes in both two and four ply. The thread is very strong and has a lovely sheen with 136 colours in the range. The thread is naturally dyed, so the same colour can never be guaranteed from one dye lot to the next. You need to make sure you buy enough material in one dyelot to complete your project.

The natural dyes of Kirra create interesting variations of colour and are particularly suitable for flowers and foliage. When I have needed stronger colours such as reds, blacks and blues, I have used Littlewood Fleece Yarns and Appletons Crewel 2 ply wools. Littlewood is a fine thread that comes in a good range of bright strong colours. Both Kirra and Littlewood are Australian products.

When using Kirra thread cut through the skein in one place and leave the tag to keep a record of the colour. Use the full length of thread when stitching. Kirra, Appleton, Littlewood and Broder Medici are best plaited into hanks and tied at both ends. The thread can then be pulled out without tangling the skein.

Do not store wool in plastic bags as it will sweat.

NEEDLES

I use numbers 5, 6 and 7 crewel needles in all the projects featured in this book. You need a sharp needle when working on wool flannel. I always use the smallest needle I can as it gives more control over the stitch size. It is very important to use a needle you are comfortable with. A tapestry needle or chenille needle may be more suitable for heavier threads.

HOOPS

It is essential to use a hoop when working some stitches to maintain an even tension. I use a 12.5 cm (5 inch) hoop bound with bias tape. When working with a hoop ensure that the screw is always at the top so that the thread will not become entangled. Keep the fabric tightly tensioned at all times.

SCISSORS

A small, good quality pair of scissors with pointed blades is essential for unpicking and snipping off threads

TAILORS CHALK

I use tailors chalk to make an outline of the design. The marks do not last long and should be stitched over with a small tacking stitch. The marks that are left are easily brushed out when the project is finished. Washable fabric markers can also be used but it is best to test these on a piece of fabric first.

TRACING PAPER

Lightweight tracing paper is best for tracing designs onto wool. Use running stitches to mark other main areas and lines of the design. Use a neutral colour wool when doing the running stitches so that the stitches will not show through when embroidered over. It is not necessary to mark all the small details. These can be copied from the pattern later. Mark the outlines, stems and flower centres. It is impossible to mark in all the details on woollen material, especially blanketing.

Working Methods

Transfer of Design to Material

It is not easy to transfer fine detail to wool flannel or blanketing. The best method is to trace the design from the printed pattern on lightweight tracing paper. Tack this pattern firmly to the fabric and work over the pattern in small running stitches. Work the main pattern lines. It may not be necessary to put in all small details. These can be copied from the printed sheet when working the embroidery.

When the design is transferred run the needle along the stitched line and pull away the paper leaving the stitched design. Details may be marked in with a wash away fabric marker. Leave the stitch guide lines on the fabric and work directly over them. They will not show. When marking the designs of the blanket in this book it may be necessary to mark only the centres of the flowers and stem lines and work the details from the printed guide.

General Notes for Working with Wool

Start with a knot and several small stitches worked on top of each other. Finish with small stitches through the back of the work. Leave a tail of wool at the back of your work 5 to 6 cm (2 to 3 inches) in length. These tails will be worked over as the embroidery progresses. The back can be tidied up when the work is finished. I don't believe in worrying too much about the look of the back as long as all the threads are secure. The back, in most cases, will be covered by the lining.

Threading the Needle

Fold the wool over, hold between the thumb and forefinger and push through the eye of the needle.

Double Threaded Needle

When working with two threads in the needle thread up two separate strands. Do not thread one strand and then double it. Using two separate pieces allows the twist of the wool to lie in the same direction. This gives the work a much more even appearance.

Outlining

The same technique is used when working the stem stitch for flowers, leaves and birds. Work the outline first in stem stitch and then fill in the area with close rows of stem stitch. Work backwards and forwards from end to end. Work the background colour first then add accents, highlights and shading over the top in either stem stitch or straight stitch.

Dryandra and Banksia (see pages 9 and 12)

Flowers like the Dryandra and Banksia are worked differently from above. The background colour is laid down first in straight stitches using an embroidery hoop. Stitches follow the direction of the shape of the design and are worked across the shape, gradually covering the area. Colour highlights, shading and shaping are built up over the top of the background until the area is fully covered.

Stitch Direction

Stitch direction should always follow the shape of the design which is being embroidered. For example, with the birds work the stitches from head to tail. The butterflies should have the stitches radiating from the body to the edge of the wings. Eucalyptus flowers have the stitches radiating from the centre and leaves have the stitches running over the length of the leaf. This helps to define the shape and add dimension to the design.

Pressing

Steam press your work lightly as you progress with the embroidery. Pad the ironing surface with a thick towel. Press lightly from the back using a high steam setting. If you have to press from the front always use a cloth to prevent a 'shiny' effect. Place a cloth over the front of the work. Then press. Leave to cool and dry thoroughly before starting further embroidery.

UNPICKING

If it is necessary to unpick your work use a small sharp pair of embroidery scissors to cut out the stitches. Once unpicked, steam press the area. Wool is wonderfully forgiving. Once pressed, an unpicked area generally does not show any marking.

SHRINKAGE

The base material will 'shrink' as it is embroidered. How much it shrinks will depend on the amount of embroidery worked on it. It is important to take this into account when embroidering garments or anything that depends on an exact pattern size. You can lose up to 3 cm (1 inch) on a heavily embroidered vest front. I allow for this by cutting the fabric slightly larger than necessary. It can be trimmed to size after the embroidery is finished and pressed.

DESIGN PROPORTION

Keep the design in proportion to the article being embroidered as well as keeping it in proportion to the subject matter. Keep the ply of the thread similar in weight to the fabric being embroidered. When embroidering knitted garments it is preferable to use a wool of similar weight or ply. Embroidering on hand knits is not recommended as a beginner's exercise!

CARE AND LAUNDERING

I recommend dry cleaning for heavily embroidered articles. The blanket in this book has been designed and worked in a simple open pattern to allow for careful hand washing.

Stitch Glossary

BULLION STITCH

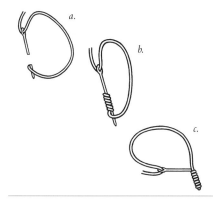

This stitch is not easy to do in wool and the thread should be changed frequently to avoid wear. The number of wraps on the needle should fill the length of the back stitch.

Make a back stitch of the required length and bring the needle up at the starting point but do not pull through. Wrap the wool around the needle in a clockwise direction. With your left thumb over the wraps pull the needle through. The stitch will turn back at this stage – pull thread firmly until it is lying flat on the fabric. Take the needle back through the fabric at the starting point and pull through.

BUTTONHOLE WHEELS AND STARS

wheel   *star*

The stitches are placed close together and can be worked in a row or a circle. By varying the length of the stitch a star can be adapted from the circle.

Starting on the outside work from left to right, hold the thread below the needle and take a downward straight stitch and pull through the fabric. Continue in this method until a wheel has been completed.

COLONIAL KNOT

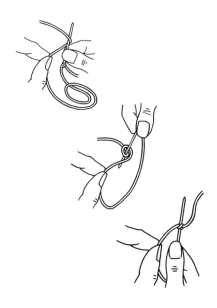

This stitch should be worked on a small hoop.

It is preferable to use this stitch rather than French knots. In most cases when working on wool fabric colonial knots stand away from the fabric more than French knots. The thread does not untwist as it does when working a large number of French knots.

1. Bring the thread through the fabric and, holding it in the left hand, hook the needle underneath.

2. Twist the needle to the left over the thread and hook back under the thread held taught in the left hand.

3. Reverse the needle direction back over the thread and enter the fabric. Pull through to the back of the fabric near the starting point.

It is important to keep tension on the thread held in the left hand until the knot is lying on the fabric as the needle is passed to the back of the work.

A half colonial knot is constructed by completing steps 1 and 2.

DETACHED CHAIN

Bring the needle through the material where you intend to start stitching. Hold the thread below the needle and insert it back into the fabric close to the starting point. Bring the needle out at the required stitch length and pull thread through. Catch down the loop formed with a small straight stitch.

FLY STITCH

A very useful stitch, it can be worked in any direction and any size. Like an open lazy-daisy stitch the tying stitch can be worked in any length. Bring the needle up at the top left, insert a small distance to the right and make a small diagonal stitch towards the centre. With the thread below the needle, pull through and tie down with a vertical stitch.

SATIN STITCH

A series of straight stitches covering the fabric completely. Work on a hoop as an even tension is very important.

STEM STITCH

A very quick stitch for stems and filling areas.

Working from left to right take even, slightly slanting stitches along the design line. Leave a half distance space between where the needle emerges and the last stitch. Keep the thread below your work.

To fill an area work outline first and then work back and forth within the outline.

STRAIGHT STITCH

A single stitch that can be worked in any direction and length. Use a hoop to keep tension even and do not make the stitches too long or they will loop when taken off the hoop.

TURKEY STITCH

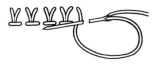

Start with the unknotted wool ends on the front of the work and anchor with a small stitch. Loop the wool below the needle and take another small stitch. Do not pull the loop through. With the wool below the needle take another small stitch to anchor the loop. Continue in this manner placing stitches close together. Fill the area to be covered then shear off the loops with small sharp scissors, then shape the pile to a realistic form.

UNCUT TURKEY STITCH

Work the same as above but do not cut loops. Both these can be worked with two or three strands in the needle to create a thicker pile.

Flower Glossary

NOTE: THE FLOWERS IN THIS CHAPTER ARE LISTED IN ALPHABETICAL ORDER ACCORDING
TO THEIR MAIN NAME, EG SILVER WATTLE, APPEARS UNDER 'W' FOR WATTLE.

PARTS OF FLOWERS

For easy reference, the drawings below refer to the parts of flowers described
in the following pages.

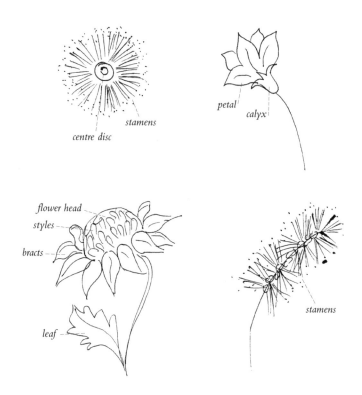

COLOURS OF FLOWERS

The descriptions of how to embroider the flowers given in this chapter do not
give details of colours. This is because some of the flowers may be used in
several projects and therefore in several different colour variations. You will
need to refer to the specific projects to find the colours and type of wool you
will need to complete the flower.

Desert Banksia (*Banksia ornata*)

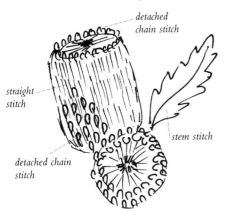

Belonging to the Protea family, a dense shrub growing to about 2.5 metres (8 feet). It flowers in autumn and winter and grows in the sandy areas of south-east South Australia and south-west Victoria.

Stitches

Straight Stitch

Detached Chain

Stem Stitch

Method

Mark an outline of the flower in a lemon-coloured wool. Place the fabric in a hoop. Fill in the marked area with straight stitches. Work backward and forward gradually filling in the entire area with vertical straight stitches. Work the top of the flower in radiating straight stitches.

Take the fabric off the frame and, with 2 strands of grey-green wool work over the straight stitched area in random detached chain stiches. Work from the bottom of the flower towards the top. With a single thread, work small detached chain stitches around the top oval area. Work the centres of the flowers in dark radiating straight stitches.

The leaves are worked in rows of stem stitch – work the serrated outline first, then fill in. The centre vein is worked in stem stitch.

Black Boy or Grass Tree (*Xanthorrhoea australis*)

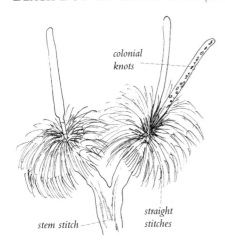

Erect shrub with a short trunk and a flowering stem to 3 metres (10 feet) high. The leaves are long, stiff and grasslike and grow in a tuft at the end of the trunk. It is very slow growing and flowers erratically, often after fire. Widespread in sandy soils in heaths and open forests of most states of Australia.

Stitches

Stem Stitch

Straight Stitch

Colonial Knots

Method

Mark the outline of the stem in running stitches and fill in with rows of stem stitch. In working tree trunks, I often use a random (dyed) thread and, to give a mottled effect, I vary the length of the row worked.

Mark the approximate area to be covered by the top of the tree in tailors chalk and place fabric in a hoop. Working from the centre of the tree, radiate stitches around the area to be filled. Make stitches approximately 2 cms (1 inch) in length and work close together to fill in area. Try to keep the outside stitches at different lengths to keep the edge of the tree light and 'feathery'.

The flower stalks are worked in rows of colonial knots using two strands of threads in the needle.

ROYAL BLUEBELL (*WAHLENBERGIA GLORIOSA*)

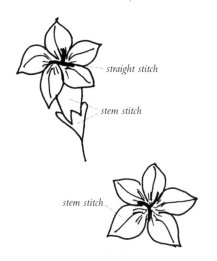

straight stitch

stem stitch

stem stitch

The Royal Bluebell is the floral emblem of the Australian Capital Territory. The flowers are solitary on long thin stalks with five delicate pointed lobes. The leaves are confined to the lower stem. Its growth is restricted to the sub-alpine woodland region of New South Wales, Victoria and Tasmania.

STITCHES

Stem Stitch

Straight Stitch

METHOD

Outline the flower petals in stem stitch in blue. Fill in the area with rows of stem stitch. Mark in the centre line of each petal with a darker blue and mark in shading around the centre with small straight stitches in the same darker colour. The centre of the flower is worked in three straight stitches in white. The buds, trumpet, calyx, stems and leaves are worked in stem stitch.

BOTTLEBRUSH (*CALLISTOMEN –)*

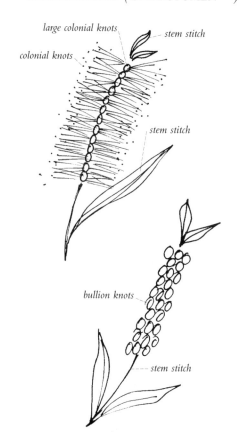

large colonial knots

stem stitch

colonial knots

stem stitch

bullion knots

stem stitch

There are many varieties of Callistomen growing wild in the Australian bush and many more cultivated varieties in Australian gardens. They come in a range of colours from deep red to pale cream.

STITCHES

Colonial Knots

Straight Stitch

Stem Stitch

Bullion Circles

METHOD

The Flower

Work in a hoop. Mark the centre line and work in large colonial knots with two strands of wool in the needle. Mark side guide lines with tailors chalk and work the stamens in straight stitches in groups of three to four stitches from the centre colonial knots. Scatter colonial knots to form pollen along the edges and through the centre of the flower.

Seed Cases

Mark the guide lines in tailors chalk. Fill in the area with bullion knots, wrapping the needle thirteen to sixteen times for each knot. Catch down each knot with a small straight stitch to make it lie flat on the surface of the fabric.

The leaves and stems are worked in stem stitch.

Cooktown Orchid (*Dendrobium bigibbum*)

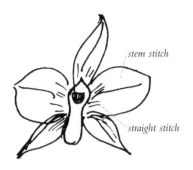

stem stitch

straight stitch

The Cooktown Orchid is the floral emblem of Queensland. It flowers most of the year and grows on trees and rocks in the rain forests. It ranges in colour from deep pink to white.

Stitches

Stem Stitch

Straight Stitch

Method

Work the outline of the petals in stem stitch in pale pink and fill in the area with stem stitch in various shades of pink. Add highlights in small straight stitches. Work labellum in stem stitch in shades of darker pink and burgundy.

Daisies

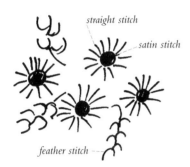

straight stitch

satin stitch

feather stitch

There are many varieties of small daisy-like flowers native to Australia. They are widely cultivated and come in a wide range of colours. These are a very useful 'filler' flower to use in many designs.

Stitches

Satin Stitch

Straight Stitch

Feather Stitch

Method

The centre is worked in satin stitch, three to five stitches with two threads in the needle. The petals are worked around the centre in straight stitches, two threads in the needle. These can also be worked in one thread of 4 ply Kirra. The number of petals can vary according to the size of the flower.

The leaves are worked in feather stitch and are placed throughout the flower spray where needed.

Sturts Desert Pea (*Clianthus formosus*)

stem stitch

straight stitch

stem stitch

stem stitch   *fly stitch*

The South Australian floral emblem—a prostrate spreading plant. The flowers are pea-shaped and bright red with a large glossy black spot at the centre. It flowers in spring in the sandy soils in arid inland areas of all states except Tasmania.

Stitches

Stem Stitch

Fly Stitch

Straight Stitch

Method

Mark the outlines with small running stitches and fill in with stem stitch. Work the centre areas in stem stitch. The black centres are worked in stem stitch and the white highlights in small straight stitches. The leaves are worked in fly stitch in a leaf shape with the stitches close together. The stems are worked in stem stitch.

Sturts Desert Rose (*Gossypium sturtianum*)

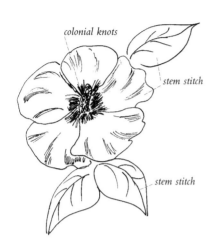

colonial knots

stem stitch

stem stitch

The floral emblem of the Northern Territory of Australia, this grows to a dense shrub 2 metres (6 feet) high. The flowers are pink or lilac with dark red centres with five overlapping petals and a protruding column of fused stamens. It flowers most of the year in arid sandy sites in gorges and gullies inland in all mainland states of Australia.

Stitches

Stem Stitch

Colonial Knots

Method

Mark the outline of the flower and leaves in small running stitches or tailors chalk. The body of the flower is worked in rows of stem stitch. Work each petal separately starting at the centre and fanning the rows towards the edge —allow the rows to follow the shape of the petal. The central stamen is worked in colonial knots.

The leaves are worked in stem stitch with the veins added over the top.

Showy Dryandra (*Dryandra formosa*)

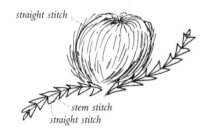

straight stitch

stem stitch
straight stitch

The Showy Dryandra is a small tree 4–8 metres (12–24 feet) with narrow leaves deeply divided into many triangular lobes. The flowers are yellow-orange with long protruding styles. It flowers in spring and is native to south-western Western Australia. It belongs to the Protea family and is widely cultivated.

Oak-Leafed Dryandra (*Dryandra quercifolia*)

straight stitch
colonial knot

stem stitch
straight stitch

Larger-flowered than the Showy Dryandra it flowers from autumn to spring and is also a native of south-west Western Australia.

Stitches

Straight Stitch

Colonial Knot

Stem Stitch

Method

Mark the outline of the flowers in running stitch and place the fabric in a hoop with tension tight. Fill the whole area of the flower in the background colour, working with straight stitches and following directional lines. Add highlight colour to define the shape of the flower. Start with the lighter colours and work to darker areas.

Oak-Leafed Dryandra flower is worked same as above with the addition of bracts worked around the flower in straight stitch. The stamens are then added in straight stitch with a colonial knot on the end.

Showy Dryandra Leaves—take the fabric out of the hoop and work the centre rib in two rows of stem stitch. Add the triangular serrations in straight stitches.

Oak-Leafed Dryandra Leaves—are worked in rows of stem stitch.

EREMAEA (BEAUFORTIOIDES)

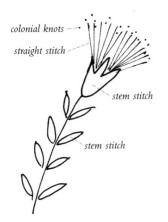

colonial knots
straight stitch
stem stitch
stem stitch

Commonly called the Broad-Leafed Eremaea. The flowers are bright orange and brush like. It is native to south-west Western Australia and flowers in the spring.

STITCHES

Stem Stitch

Straight Stitch

Colonial Knot

METHOD

Work the calyx in stem stitch first. Place the material in a hoop with the tension tight and work the stamens in long straight stitches radiating from an imaginary centre in the calyx. Scatter pollen dust at the end of the long stitches in colonial knots.

Take the fabric off the hoop. Work the stems and leaves in stem stitch.

EUCALYPTUS FLOWERS

straight stitch
buttonhole stitch

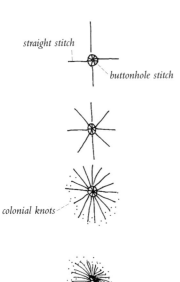

colonial knots

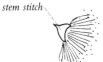

stem stitch

There are many hundreds of eucalyptus species. The flowers are all similar in that they comprise a central disc surrounded by many long stamens. The colour, size and shape of the woody calyxes and seed pods vary greatly.

STITCHES

Buttonhole Stitch

Straight Stitch

Colonial Knot

Half Colonial Knot

Stem Stitch

Uncut Turkey Stitch

METHOD

Flower

Mark the centres and work in buttonhole rings. Work the stems in stem stitch and calyxes of half flowers in stem stitches.

Place the fabric in a hoop with the tension tight. Work the stamens in straight stitch, radiating from the buttonhole centre. (With the large flowers on the waistcoats it may be necessary to vary the length of the stitches. Do not make the stitches too long or they will loop when taken off the hoop.) Work in sections around the centre to avoid a spiral effect. Gradually build up the stitch density.

Follow the direction of the stitch to create the shape of the flower.

After the stamens have been worked, scatter colonial and half colonial knots to create the pollen.

EUCALYPTUS LEAVES

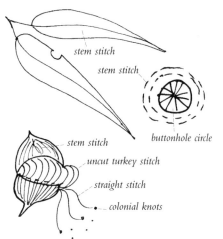

stem stitch

stem stitch

buttonhole circle

stem stitch

uncut turkey stitch

straight stitch

colonial knots

Work the outline in stem stitch and then fill in with rows of stem stitch working from the outside towards the centre. Don't forget the caterpillar bites! Work the centre vein last in stem stitch. The stems and branches are worked in stem stitch.

Buds

Opening buds are worked in stem stitch and uncut turkey stitch with a scattering of colonial knots. Work the two sides of the bud first then fill area in between with uncut turkey stitch. Several long stamens can be added in straight stitch. Couch them into curved shapes for a more natural look.

Woody Fruits

Work centre disc in buttonhole circle and add rows of stem stitch around this until it is the required size.

BLUNT EVERLASTING (HELICHRYSUM OBRUSIFOLIUM)

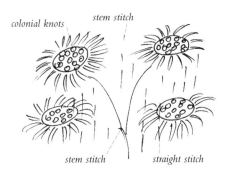

colonial knots

stem stitch

stem stitch

straight stitch

Upright perennial to 40 cms (16 inches) with straight, grey-green stems. Flowers are white composite daisy-like with a yellow centre. They flower in spring and are widespread in the sandy soils and open heaths of New South Wales, Victoria, South Australia and Western Australia.

STITCHES
Colonial Knots

Straight Stitch

Stem Stitch

METHOD
Mark the centres and work in colonial knots with two threads of 2 ply in the needle. The petals are worked in tapestry wool in long straight stitches radiating from the centres. Fill in the area between the flowers with parallel rows of stem stitch to create a background of stems and leaves.

FLANNEL FLOWER (ACTINOTUS HELIANTHI)

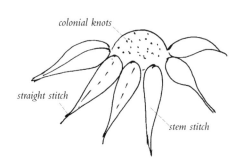

colonial knots

straight stitch

stem stitch

An upright annual plant covered in woolly hairs. The flowers are white, the petals tipped in green and covered in dense soft hairs. It may have between ten and eighteen petals. The Flannel Flower grows in sandy soils along the coast and ranges of Queensland and New South Wales.

STITCHES
Colonial Knots

Stem Stitch

Straight Stitch

METHOD
Work the outline of the petals and fill in with stem stitch. Work the petal tips and centre highlights in straight stitch. The centre vein is worked in a broken line of straight stitch which is barely visible behind the stem stitch petals.

Place the material in the hoop with the tension tight and work the centre in colonial knots. Pile up the stitches against each other to create a raised effect. The leaves are worked in stem stitch.

Fringe Lily *(Thysanotus Tuberosus)*

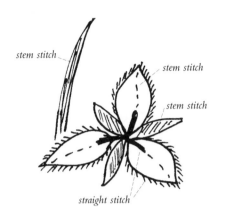

stem stitch

stem stitch

stem stitch

straight stitch

The flowers range from blue to purple in colour and are between 15–35 cm (6–14 inches) across. It blooms in spring and summer and is widespread in grassland areas of the eastern states of Australia.

Stitches

Stem Stitch

Straight Stitch

Method

Outline the large petals in stem stitch and then fill in with rows of stem stitch. Work around the petals with tiny straight stitches to form the fringe. The centre lines, smaller petals and stems are worked in stem stitch. Centres are worked in straight stitch.

Work the larger petals first, then the smaller petals and finally the centres.

Geraldton Wax Flower *(Chameleiucium Uncinatum)*

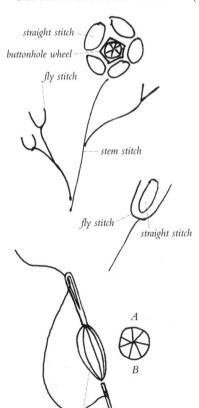

straight stitch

buttonhole wheel

fly stitch

stem stitch

fly stitch

straight stitch

A

B

straight stitch

A shrubby plant growing to a height of 5 metres (15 feet). The flowers cover the bush thickly and range in colour from white to deep red. It flowers in spring and summer and is native to the limestone coastal areas of Western Australia.

Stitches

Fly Stitch

Straight Stitch

Buttonhole Stitch

Stem Stitch

Method

Flower

Work the centres of the flowers in buttonhole stitch. The petals are worked in straight stitch with two threads in the needle. Build up the petal, working five or six stitches over the top of each other—entering and leaving the fabric at the same spot. Work the stitches horizontal to the centre. Keep the tension of the stitch fairly loose and allow the thread to fall to either side of the petal.

Buds

The buds are worked similarly to the petals: several straight stitches 'built up' on top of each other. A fly stitch is worked around each bud.

Leaves

The leaves are long fly stitches attached to stems.

SHOWY GROUNDSEL (*SENECIO MAGNIFICUS*)

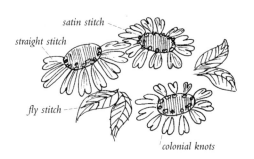

The flowers are yellow to orange in terminal clusters of 10–50 on long branching stems. They are daisy-like with 6–10 large rays and flower in spring in creekbeds in dry inland areas of all mainland states.

STITCHES

Satin Stitch

Straight Stitch

Fly Stitch

Colonial Knots

METHOD

Mark the centres and work in satin stitch. The petals are worked in tapestry wool with four long straight stitches to each petal radiating from the centre. Scatter colonial knots around the area where the petals join the centres.

Leaves are fly stitches packed lightly together.

COMMON HEATH (*EPACRIS IMPRESSA*)

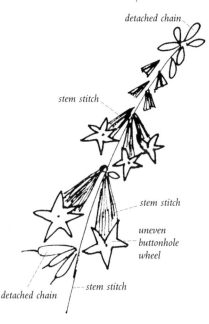

The floral emblem of Victoria. It grows in wet soils in the heaths and woodlands of the coast and tablelands of New South Wales, Victoria, Tasmania and South Australia. The flowers are pink to red, rarely white in colour. They are arranged in leafy spikes to 2 metres (6 feet) high. Heath flowers for most of the year and is cultivated as a native garden plant.

STITCHES

Stem Stitch

Detached Chain

Uneven Buttonhole Wheel

METHOD

Work the centre stem lines in stem stitch. Add the top leaves in detached chain stitch. Starting at the top of the stem work the flower tubes in stem stitch. Work the 'stars' at the base of the flower tubes in buttonhole stars. Fill in leaves in detached chain stitches along the length of the stem where space allows. Attach the flowers to the stem with small detached chain stitches.

Tea Tree *(Leptospermum –)*

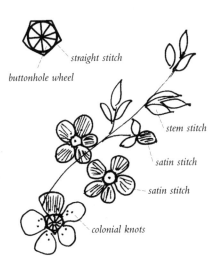

straight stitch

buttonhole wheel

stem stitch

satin stitch

satin stitch

colonial knots

There are many varieties of Tea Tree throughout Australia. The flowers are all similar in structure—five petals around a central disc. The colours vary from white to deep red and they are widely cultivated as a garden plant.

Stitches

Satin Stitch

Buttonhole Wheels

Stem Stitch

Straight Stitch

Colonial Knots

Method

Work the stems first in stem stitch, the flower centres next in buttonhole wheels and the five petals around the centre in satin stitch. Work a straight stitch at the base of each petal around the centre in deep red. Scatter colonial knots around the centre of the larger flowers. Leaves are worked at random between the flowers, along the stems in stem stitch.

Kangaroo Apple *(Solanum sturtium)*

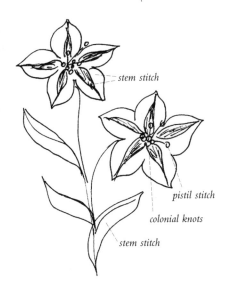

stem stitch

pistil stitch

colonial knots

stem stitch

An erect shrub to 3 metres (10 feet). The leaves are silvery green and covered with downy hairs. The flowers are mauve to purple with five papery petals and five yellow stamens. It flowers from autumn to spring in all dry inland areas.

Stitches

Straight Stitch

Pistil Stitch

Stem Stitch

Colonial Knot

Method

Mark outline of flowers and fill in with stem stitch in lighter colour. Add the deeper-coloured centre markings in straight stitch. The centres are worked in straight stitch and colonial knots.

Stem and leaves are worked in stem stitch.

Mangle Kangaroo Paw (Anigozanthos Manglesii)

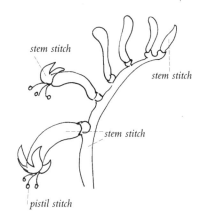

The floral emblem of Western Australia. It grows to 1 metre (3 feet) high. The flowers are tubular green and red with six curled back lobes on one side. They are arranged in terminal racemes and a hairy red stem.

Stitches

Stem Stitch

Pistil Stitch

Method

This flower is worked in stem stitch. The stamens are worked in pistil stitch and the 'turn back' petals in pale green stem stitch.

Parakeelya (Calandrinia Remota)

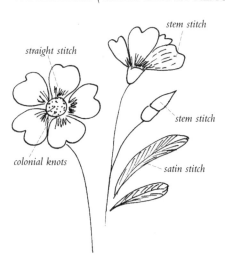

A low, semi-prostrate herb with many flowering stems to 50 cms (20 inches) long. The flowers are mauve pink to purple with a whitish yellow centre and five open petals, notched at the tips. It flowers for most of the year in the sandy, arid areas of the Northern Territory, Queensland, South Australia and Western Australia.

Stitches

Stem Stitch

Straight Stitch

Colonial Knots

Satin Stitch

Method

Mark outline of flower and fill in petals with rows of stem stitch. Work from the centre outwards. Add deeper highlights in straight stitch.

Centres are worked in colonial knots and the leaves in satin stitch.

Showy Parrot Pea (Dillwynia Sericea)

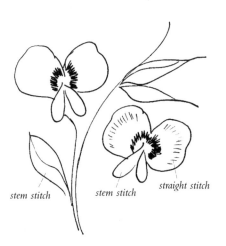

A bushy shrub to 1.5 metres (4 1/2 feet) high. The flowers are pea-shaped, yellow or orange, often with a red centre. They have a kidney-shaped standard petal and flower in spring in the woodlands in the tablelands and ranges of Queensland, New South Wales, South Australia, Victoria and Tasmania.

Stitches

Stem Stitch

Straight Stitch

Method

The flower is worked in a hoop. Mark the kidney-shaped main petals and fill in with small straight stitches working from the centre outwards. Add highlights in straight stitches around the centre of the flower. The lower petals are worked in stem stitch as are leaves.

POACHED EGG DAISIES (MYRIOCEPHALUS STUARTII)

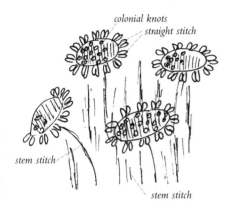

An erect woolly herb to 60 cms (2 feet) high, flowers are white composite buttons with a large yellow centre. It flowers in spring and summer in the mallee sandhills of inland Australia.

STITCHES

Colonial Knots

Straight Stitch

Stem Stitch

METHOD

Mark the centre of the daisies with pencil or tailors chalk and work over the area in long straight stitches. Cover over these stitches with colonial knots using two threads in the needle or tapestry wool. The petals are small straight stitches worked in pairs around the centre. Fill in areas around and between the flowers with stem stitch leaves.

GOLDEN WATTLE (ACACIA PYCNANTHA)

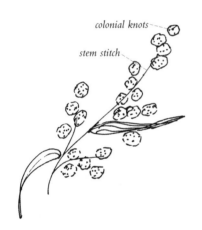

The Golden Wattle is Australia's floral emblem. The flowers are tightly-packed golden fluffy balls sometimes entirely covering the tree. It flowers in winter and late spring and is widespread in open forest areas of New South Wales, Victoria, South Australia and Western Australia.

STITCHES

Stem Stitch

Colonial Knots

Detached Chain

METHOD

Work the stems in stem stitch. Place the fabric in the hoop and tension tightly. Work the flowers in colonial knots packed together tightly to form rounded balls. Remove fabric from the hoop to work the leaves in stem stitch.

SILVER WATTLE

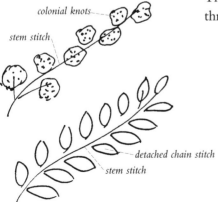

The leaves of the Silver Wattle are worked in detached chain stitch with two threads in the needle.

Wattle—method 3

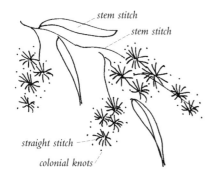

stem stitch
stem stitch
straight stitch
colonial knots

Stitches

Stem Stitch

Straight Stitch

Colonial Knots

Method

In this version of the wattle, work the stems and leaves in stem stitch first.

The flowers are worked on a hoop using radiating small straight stitches. When a round shape is obtained, scatter colonial and half colonial or French Knots randomly around the outside of the flower. Make the flowers smaller as they progress along the stems towards the tips.

Waratah (Telopea speciosissima)

detached chain stitch
stem stitch
stem stitch

The New South Wales floral emblem grows to four metres (12 feet) high. The flowers are crimson and arranged in dense compact globular heads 8–15 cms (3–6 inches) in diameter and surrounded by red bracts. It flowers in spring and grows in the sandy coastal soils of New South Wales.

Stitches

Straight Stitch

Stem Stitch

Detached Chain Stitch

Method

This flower is worked in a similar manner to the Desert Banksia. After marking in the outline of the flower, place the fabric in the hoop. Fill in the body of the flower with rows of straight stitches following stitch direction guide. Work the top of the flower in radiating straight stitches. Work over these stitches in the same colour using two strands of thread in the needle in rows of detached chain stitches. Add random stitches in pink.

The bracts are worked in stem stitch. Leaves are also worked in rows of stem stitch—do the outline first then fill in working towards the centre. Add veins in stem stitch last of all.

Native Wisteria (*Hardenbergia comptoniana*)

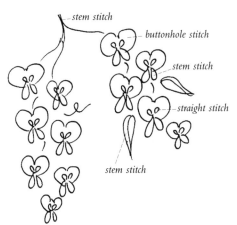

stem stitch

buttonhole stitch

stem stitch

straight stitch

stem stitch

Flowers in winter and spring with mauve to blue, pink or white pea-shaped flowers arranged in long racemes. A vigorous climber, it is native to Western Australia.

Stitches

Buttonhole Stitch

Stem Stitch

Straight Stitch

Satin Stitch

Method

Mark the position of the flowers and approximate shape with chalk or pencil.

The large petals of the flower are worked in buttonhole stitch radiating from a central point. Vary the stitch length to create the correct shape of the two large petals. The two front petals are worked in detached chain stitch and the small green spots in satin stitch. The stems and leaves are worked in stem stitch. The buds are worked in stem stitch.

Captions for Colour Plates

PLATE 1   23

PLATE 3   25

PLATE 5 27

PLATE 7 29

PLATE 9   31

PLATE 11 *33*

Projects

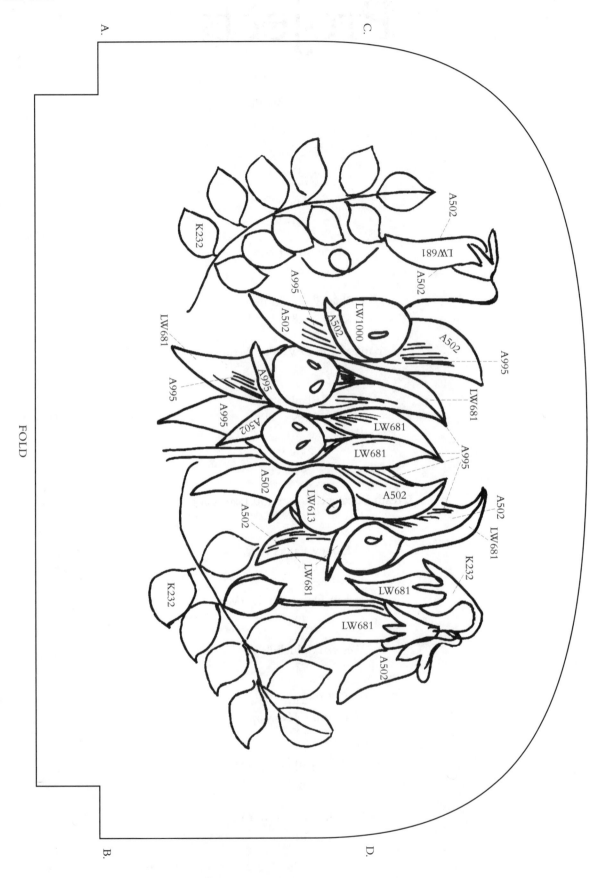

Sturt Desert Pea Purse

METHOD

1. Transfer the design to the fabric. Mark an outline of the purse shape with a fabric marker. Do not cut out.
2. Embroider the design using the directions in the flower glossary and following the colour guide.

CONSTRUCTION OF PURSE

1. Press embroidery lightly and remark the purse shape. Cut out.
2. Cut the lining and wadding the same size as the purse shape.
3. Tack the three pieces of fabric together.
4. Bind the raw edges from points A to B on both ends.
5. On the inside slip stitch points A to C and points B to D.
6. Tack in the zipper from points C to D and then hand stitch into place. Sew in the other side of the zipper, leaving the zipper open.
7. Turn to the right side and check the zipper. Turn the purse inside out and sew across the bottom open edges making a box bottom to the purse. Neaten the inside seam using a zig zag stitch. Turn to the right side.

THREADS	NUMBERS
LITTLEWOOD 2PLY	681 x 1
LITTLEWOOD 2PLY	1000 x 1
LITTLEWOOD 2PLY	613 x 1
APPLETON 2PLY	502 x 1
APPLETON 2PLY	995 x 1
KIRRA 2PLY	232 x 1

FLOWER

Sturt Desert Pea

STITCHES

Stem Stitch
Fly Stitch
Straight Stitch

MATERIALS

black wool crepe,
35cm x 35 cm
(14" x 14")
black taffeta lining,
35 cm x 35 cm
(14" x 14")
bonded wadding
bias—black satin or cut
from lining, 1m (1 yard)
zipper, black
size 30 cm (12")
fabric marker

Tea Cosy

THREADS	NUMBERS	THREADS	NUMBERS
BOTTLEBRUSH		**FLANNEL FLOWER**	
LITTLEWOOD 2PLY	681 x 1	*Petals*	
APPLETON 2PLY	A 502 x 1	KIRRA 2PLY	330 x 1
KIRRA 2PLY	105 x 1	KIRRA 2PLY	232 x 1
KIRRA 2PLY	214 x 1	*Centre markings on petals*	
		KIRRA 2PLY	214 x 1
WATTLE		*Tips of petals and centres*	
KIRRA 2PLY	105 x 1	KIRRA 2PLY	231 x 1
KIRRA 2PLY	232 x 1		
		STURT DESERT PEA	
EUCALYPTUS		APPLETON 2PLY	502 x 1
Centres		LITTLEWOOD 2PLY	681 x 1
KIRRA 2PLY	108 x 1	LITTLEWOOD 2PLY	1000 x 1
Stamens		APPLETON 2PLY	995 x 1
KIRRA 2PLY	103 x 1		
Pollen		**BUTTERFLY**	
KIRRA 2 PLY	330 x 1	*Wings*	
		KIRRA 2PLY	330 x 1
		Shading on the wings	
		KIRRA 2 PLY	105 x 1
		LITTLEWOOD 2PLY	1000 x 1
		APPLETON	581 x 1

Tea Cosy

METHOD

1. Cut a piece of wool flannel to size 30 cm x 40 cm (12" x 16").

2. Mark outline of the pattern on the wool flannel with a washout marker or tailor's chalk.

3. Transfer the design to the fabric (see page 4).

4. Work the embroidery following the instructions in the flower glossary and following the stitch and colour guide. The butterfly wings are worked in stem stitch. The background colour is worked first, followed by the black markings and by the yellow shading over the top. The body is worked after the wings are completed in cut turkey stitch. Use one black thread and one brown thread in the needle for this stitch. The body is then trimmed to shape. Make sure you use a sharp pair of embroidery scissors for this procedure and clip to a rounded body shape. Work the antenna in stem stitch with a colonial knot at the end.

5. Steam press.

CONSTRUCTION OF TEA COSY

1. Cut out four pattern shapes in wool flannel, making one of them from the embroidered fabric.

2. Cut two shapes in wool wadding.

3. With right sides together place the wool wadding on top of embroidery piece.

4. Machine stitch around the edge leaving an opening to turn from A to B.

5. Clip the seams and turn to the right side. Sew up the openings. Press.

6. Make the back in the same manner.

7. Pin two pieces together right sides out. Slip stitch from B to C using one strand of wool in a colour to match the fabric.

8. Sew on ribbons at the marked places. Slip stitch to the bottom edge. Steam press.

SLIPPERS

The slippers included in our photograph with the tea cosy were purchased and embroidered using the same flowers and stitches, reduced and positioned to fit.

FLOWERS

Bottle Brush
Eucalyptus
Wattle
Flannel Flower
Sturt Desert Pea

STITCHES

Straight Stitch
Stem Stitch
Colonial Knot
Detached Chain
Turkey Stitch

MATERIALS

*navy wool flannel,
size 30 cm x 40 cm
(12" x 16")*

*wool wadding, 2 pieces
each, size 30 x 40 cm
(12" x 16")*

*matching or contrasting
ribbon, 1 m (1 yard)*

*embroidery hoop,
12.5 cm (5")*

crewel needles, no. 5

embroidery scissors

dressmaking scissors

washout marker

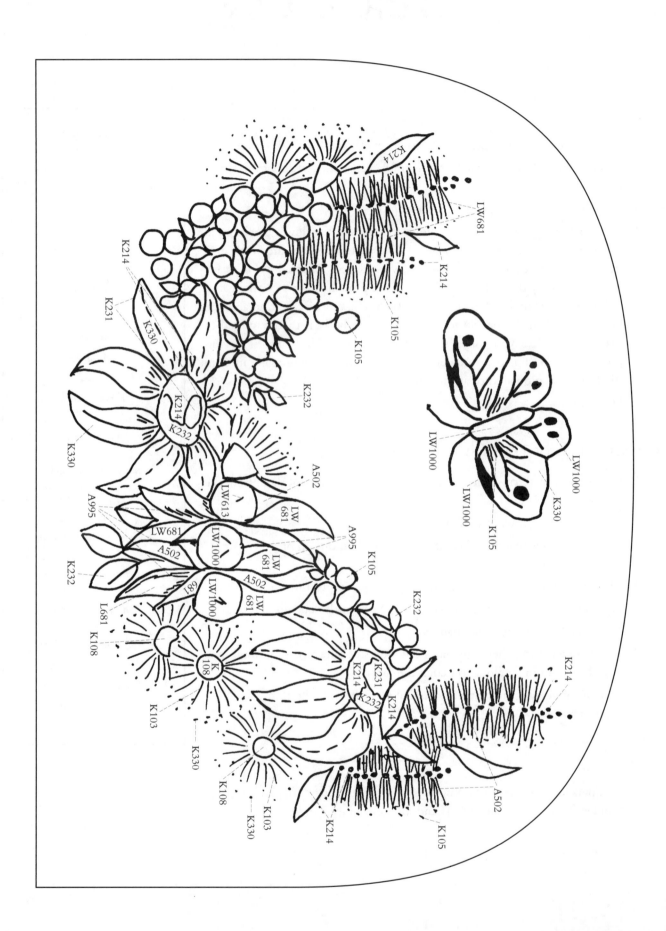

Beret

Threads	Numbers
Wattle	
Leaves	
KIRRA 2PLY	219 x 1
Stem	
KIRRA 2PLY	128 x 1
Flowers	
KIRRA 2PLY	104 x 1
Heath	
Stems and leaves	
KIRRA 2PLY	207 x 1
Stars	
KIRRA 2PLY	330 x 1
Trumpets	
KIRRA 2PLY	307 x 1
Eucalypts	
Centres and leaves	
KIRRA 2PLY	208 x 1
Stamens	
KIRRA 2PLY	102 x 1
Pollen	
KIRRA 2PLY	330 x 1
Desert Pea	
Leaves	
KIRRA 2PLY	232 x 1
Centre	
LITTLEWOOD	1000 x 1
Highlights	
KIRRA 2PLY	613 x 1
Petals	
LITTLEWOOD	681 x 1
APPLETON	502 x 1
	995 x 1

Threads	Numbers
Flannel Flowers	
Petals	
KIRRA 2PLY	330 x 1
	232 x 1
	214 x 1
	231 x 1
Bottlebrush	
Dark Stamen	
APPLETONS	502 x 1
Light Stamen	
LITTLEWOOD	681 x 1
Pollen	
KIRRA 2PLY	104 x 1
Leaves	
KIRRA 2PLY	214 x 1
Centre dots	
KIRRA 2PLY	214 x 1
Geraldton Wax	
Stems	
KIRRA 2PLY	209 x 1
Leaves	
KIRRA 2PLY	209 x 1
Centre	
KIRRA 2PLY	308 x 1
Petals	
KIRRA 2PLY	307, 302 x 1
Daisies	
Petals	
KIRRA 2PLY	101 x 1
Centre	
KIRRA 2PLY	128 x 1

Beret

METHOD

1. If you are using a lined beret on which to work the embroidery you will need to open part of the inside lining. Unpick the stitching around the circumference of the centre lining and tack back raw edges to prevent fraying.

2. Transfer the design onto the beret using the prescribed method. See page 4.

3. Work the embroidery following directions in the flower glossary and using the colour stitch guide chart.

4. Steam press lightly from the wrong side.

5. Sew up opening of the lining of the beret using small slip stitches

FLOWERS

Wattle
Pink Heath
Eucalypt
Sturt Desert Pea
Flannel Flower
Bottle Brush
Geraldton Wax

STITCHES

Colonial Knots
Stem Stitch
Straight Stitch
Button Hole Wheels
Feather Stitch
Detached Chain

MATERIALS

Purchased velvet or
flannel beret
Embroidery hoop,
12.5cm (5")
Crewel needle, size 5
Embroidery scissors

Drawstring Bag

THREADS	NUMBERS
DARK WATTLE	
Flowers	
KIRRA 2PLY	105 x 1
Stems and leaves	
KIRRA 2PLY	213 x 1
LIGHT WATTLE	
Flowers	
KIRRA 2PLY	103 x 1
KIRRA 2PLY	232 x 1
RED EUCALYPTUS	
Flowers / Stamens	
LITTLEWOOD 2PLY	681 x 1
LITTLEWOOD 2PLY	502 x 1
Pollen	
KIRRA 2PLY	105 x 1
Centre	
KIRRA 2PLY	106 x 1
Leaves	
KIRRA 2PLY	114 x 1
DAISIES	
Centre	
KIRRA 2PLY	128 x 1
Petals	
KIRRA 2PLY	331 x 2
PINK EUCALYPTUS	
Stamens	
LITTLEWOOD 2PLY	16 x 1
	17 x 1
Leaves, stems and centres	
KIRRA 2PLY	232 x 1
BOTTLE BRUSH	
Stamens	
KIRRA 2PLY	106 x 1
Pollen	
KIRRA 2PLY	105 x 1
Leaves and centre stem	
KIRRA 2 PLY	213 x 1

THREADS	NUMBERS
FRINGED LILY	
Large petals	
DMC BM	8331 x 1
Small petals	
DMC BM	8333 x 1
Leaves	
KIRRA 2PLY	231 x 1
Stamens	
KIRRA 2PLY	105 x 1
STURT DESERT PEA	
Petals	
LITTLEWOOD 2PLY	681 x 1
APPLETON 2PLY	502 x 1
	995 x 1
Centre	
LITTLEWOOD	1000 x 1
Highlight	
LITTLEWOOD	613 x 1
Leaves	
KIRRA	232 x 1
ROYAL BLUEBELL	
Petals	
APPLETON	740 x 1
Shading	
DMC BM	6688 x 1
White centre	
LITTLEWOOD 2PLY	613 x 1
Leaves and stems	
KIRRA 2PLY	214 x 1
COOKTOWN ORCHID	
Petals	
KIRRA 2PLY	303 x 1
Shading on petals	
KIRRA 2PLY	304 x 1
Stems and leaves	
KIRRA 2PLY	213 x 1
Centre	
APPLETON	145 x 1

Drawstring Bag

METHOD

1. Zig zag round the edge of the wool flannel.
2. Transfer the pattern from the design (see page 4).
3. Embroider following the directions in the flower glossary and the colour guide.
4. Steam press.

CONSTRUCTION OF DRAWSTRING BAG

1. Sew the short sides of lining piece together. Gather the long edge to form bottom of the bag and sew to the lining circle. Turn in the top edge and press down 2 cm (1 inch). Repeat this process for the wool flannel pieces.
2. Trim bonded wadding circle to fit the inside bottom of the wool bag. Slip stitch to the bottom seam of the flannel circle. Turn down the top 2 cm (1 inch) of the flannel and press.
3. Place the bag and the lining with the wrong sides together. Slip stitch along the top edges. Place two rows of machine stitching through both layers of fabric, 4 cm (1 3/4 inches) from the top and 1 cm (1/3 inch) apart.
4. Open the side seams of the bag between the rows to make a small hole on each side of the bag. Stitch around both openings in buttonhole stitch.
5. Thread two one metre (one yard) cords through the holes. Knot the ends and pull up.

FLOWERS

Wattle
Eucalyptus
Daisies
Desert Pea
Bottle Brush
Fringe Lily
Cooktown Orchid

STITCHES

Stem Stitch
Straight Stitch
Colonial Knot
Buttonhole Wheels

MATERIALS

black wool flannel,
60 cm x 30 cm
(24" x 12")
black taffeta lining
size, 60 cm x 30 cm
(24" x 12")
black cord, 2 metres
(2 yards)
piece of wool fabric
cut to circle,
diameter 12.5 cm (5")
lining, circle,
diameter 12.5 cm (5")
bonded wadding, circle,
diameter 12.5 cm (5")

JOIN TWO HALVES OF PATTERN HERE

TOP

JOIN TWO HALVES OF PATTERN HERE

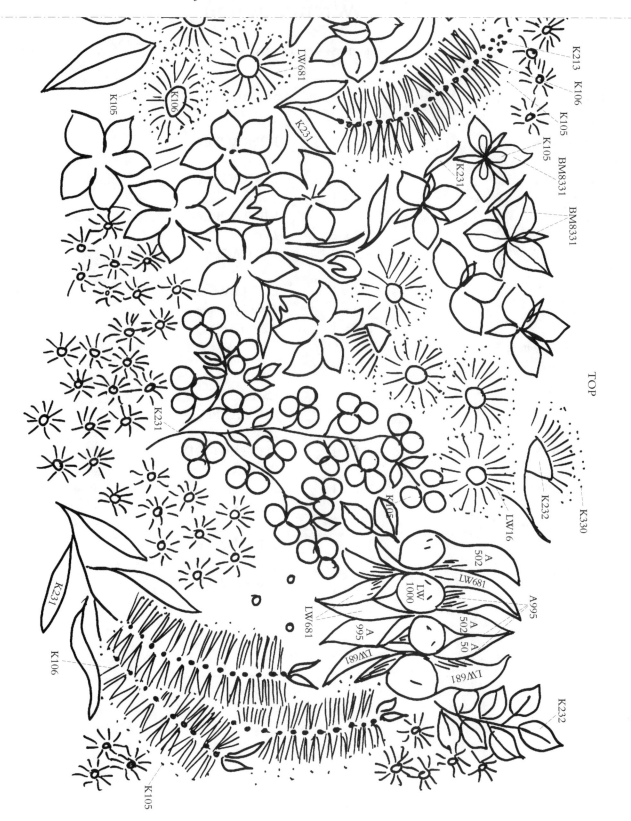

Blue Wren Cushion

THREADS	NUMBERS	THREADS	NUMBERS
TEA TREE		**MALE BIRDS**	
Stems		*Stomach*	
KIRRA 2PLY	128 x 1	KIRRA 2PLY	331 x 1
Centres		*Wing*	
KIRRA 2PLY	113 x 1	KIRRA 2PLY	128 x 1
KIRRA 2PLY	204 x 1	*Tail*	
Petals		KIRRA 2PLY	429 x 1
KIRRA 2PLY	302 x 2	*Leg*	
KIRRA 2PLY	303 x 2	KIRRA 2PLY	133 x 1
Leaves		*Chest*	
KIRRA 2PLY	204 x 1	LITTLEWOOD 2PLY	259 x 1
	209 x 1	*Light blue patches*	
	113 x 1	APPLETON	462 x 1
Stitch around centres		**FEMALE BIRDS**	
APPLETON	995 x 1	*Chest*	
HEATH		KIRRA 2PLY	331 x 1
Stems and leaves		*Back*	
KIRRA 2PLY	201 x 1	LITTLEWOOD	1000 x 1
Trumpets		KIRRA 2PLY	128 x 1
KIRRA 2PLY	307 x 1	*Eye patch*	
	308 x 1	KIRRA 2PLY	121 x 1
		Tail	
STAR		KIRRA 2PLY	127 x 1
KIRRA 2PLY	330 x 1	*Leg*	
	307 x 1	KIRRA 2PLY	133 x 1
	302 x 1		

Blue Wren Cushion

BLUE WRENS (SUPERB FAIRY WRENS) BREED PROLIFICALLY IN MY GARDEN AND HAVE BECOME VERY TAME.
AS THE YOUNG MALES OF THE PRECEDING GENERATION STAY WITH THEIR PARENTS TO HELP FEED THE PRESENT NESTLINGS
THERE IS ALWAYS A LARGE NUMBER OF THEM HOPPING AROUND THE SHRUBBERY.

METHOD

1. Cut the wool into two pieces each 40 cm x 40 cm (16" x 16").

2. Transfer the design. When transferring this design onto the material it is not necessary to mark all the details of the design. Mark in the main details of the birds, stems, larger leaves and the trumpets of the heath and the centres of the tea tree.

3. Embroider the design following the directions in the stitch glossary. Use the colour guide and follow the diagram as to the placement of the leaves and stars.

4. The birds are all worked in stem stitch. Work the stitches in the direction of the feathers ie. from beak to tail. Place one colonial knot for the eye.

5. The flowers and leaves are worked in random colours of pinks and greens.

CONSTRUCTION OF BLUE WREN CUSHION

To make up your embroidered cushion cut a piece of matching fabric for the back. Cut this piece into two. Sew together 3 cm (1 1/2 inches) from each end. Insert the zipper into the opening. Trim both pieces to 37.5 cm (15 inches) square. Sew piping in place along seam line and, with piping to the inside, place back and front together (right sides facing) and sew around all sides. Trim the corners also. Turn to right side through the zipper opening. Press and insert a cushion fill.

BIRDS

Blue Wrens
Flowers
Pink Heath
Tea Tree

STITCHES

Buttonhole Wheels
and Stars
Stem Stitch
Straight Stitch
Detached Chain
Colonial Knot

MATERIALS

Grey wool boucle,
80 cm x 40 cm
(32" x 16")
grey zipper,
35 cm (14")
pink piping,
1.5 m (1 1/2 yards)

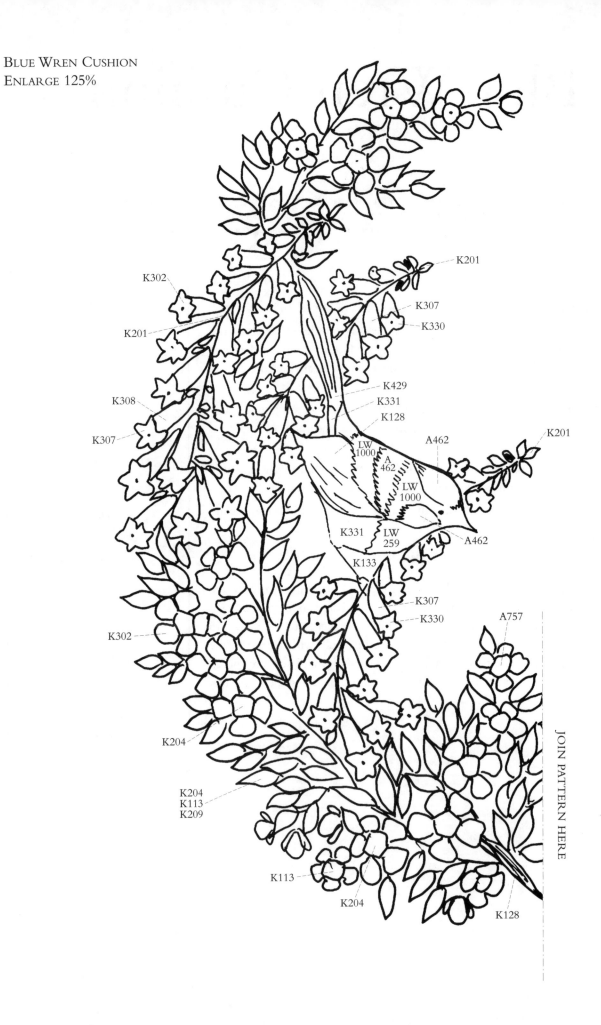

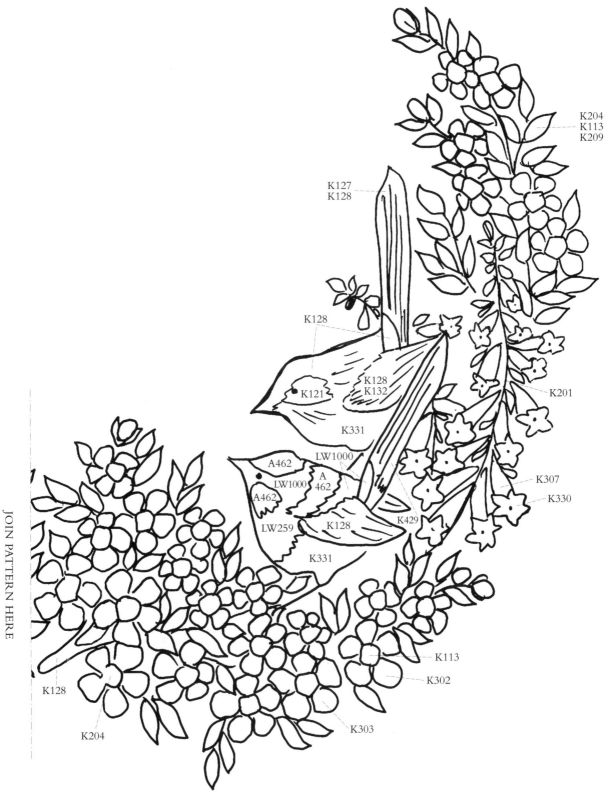

K204
K113
K209

K127
K128

K128

K128
K132

K201

K121

K331

LW1000

A462

LW1000

A
462

K307

A462

K330

LW259

K128

K429

K331

JOIN PATTERN HERE

K113

K302

K128

K204

K303

Banksia and Dryandra Picture

THREADS	NUMBERS	THREADS	NUMBERS
BOTTLEBRUSH		**BANKSIA**	
Stems and leaves		*Background*	
KIRRA 2PLY	219 x 1	KIRRA 2PLY	102 x 1
Stamens		*Top circle*	
KIRRA 2PLY	101 x 1	KIRRA 2PLY	103 x 1
Pollen		*Centres*	
KIRRA 2PLY	103 x 1	KIRRA 2PLY 128 x 1	
Seed cases		*Detached chain accents*	
KIRRA 2PLY	133 x 1	KIRRA 2PLY	222 x 1
		Leaves	
DRYANDRA		LITTLEWOOD 2PLY	6 x 1
Background colour, middle ring			
KIRRA 2PLY	103 x 1	**EREMEA**	
Accent, background on outer ring		*Stamens*	
KIRRA 2PLY	105 x 1	KIRRA 2PLY	126 x 1
Centre ring, accent on outer ring		KIRRA 2PLY	124 x 1
KIRRA 2PLY	106 x 1	KIRRA 2PLY	121 x 1
Bracts		*Pollen*	
KIRRA 2PLY	126 x 1	KIRRA 2PLY	106 x 1
Green brown leaves		*Leaves and calyx*	
LITTLEWOOD	7 x 1	LITTLEWOOD 2PLY	6 x 1
SMALL DRYANDRA		**BUTTERFLY**	
Background colours		*Body and wings accents*	
KIRRA 2PLY	106 x 1	LITTLEWOOD 2PLY	1000 x 1
	105 x 1		613 x 1
	103 x 1	KIRRA 2PLY	125 x 1
Accent colours and centres		*Wing colour*	
KIRRA 2PLY	125 x 1	KIRRA 2PLY	106 x 1
Leaves			
KIRRA 2PLY	219 x 1		
LITTLEWOOD 2 PLY	6 x 1		

Banksia and Dryandra Picture

METHOD

1. Transfer the design onto the fabric (see page 4).
2. Embroider the design following the directions in the flower glossary and colour guide.

BUTTERFLY EMBROIDERY

The wings are worked in stem stitch. I find it easier to work all the black areas first and then fill in with the colours. The body is worked in turkey stitch and trimmed into shape using small sharp scissors. Clip to a 'velvety' texture. The antennae are worked in stem stitch with a colonial knot on the end.

FRAMING

You have gone to so much trouble to make this picture that it is well worth the effort to have it professionally framed.

FLOWERS

Banksia
Dryandra
Bottlebrush
Eremea
Butterfly

STITCHES

Straight Stitch
Stem Stitch
Bullion Stitch
Detached Chain
Colonial Knots
Turkey Stitch

MATERIALS

Wool flannel, caramel colour, 40 cm x 40 cm (16" x 16") frame and mounts, or preferably have professionally framed

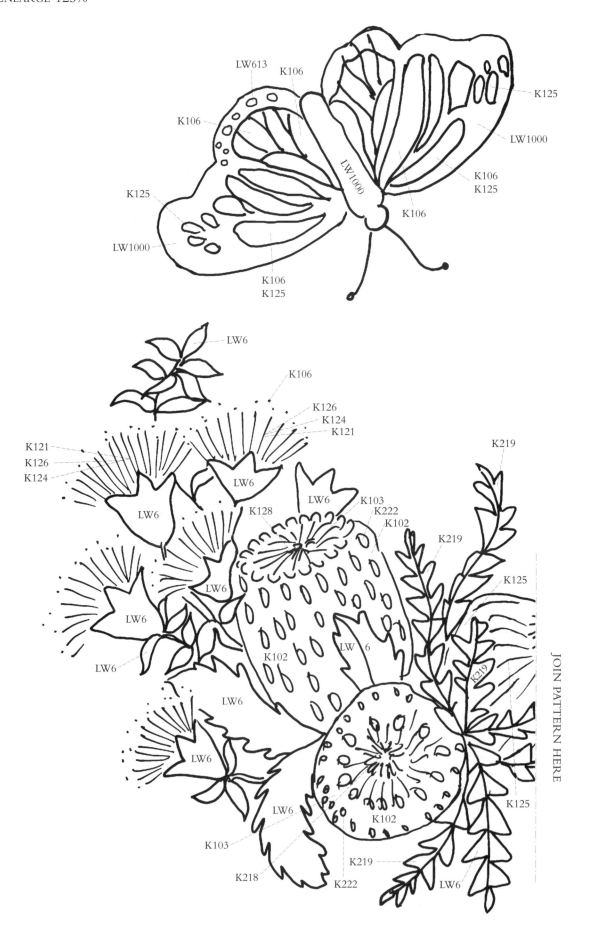

LW613
K106
K106
K125
LW1000
K106
K125
K106
K125
K106
LW1000
K106
K106
K125
LW1000
LW1000

LW6
K106
K126
K124
K121
K121
K126
K124
LW6
LW6
LW6
K128
LW6
K103
K222
K102
K219
K219
K125
LW6
LW6
K102
LW 6
K219
K102
K103
K219
K218
K222
K125
LW6
LW6

JOIN PATTERN HERE

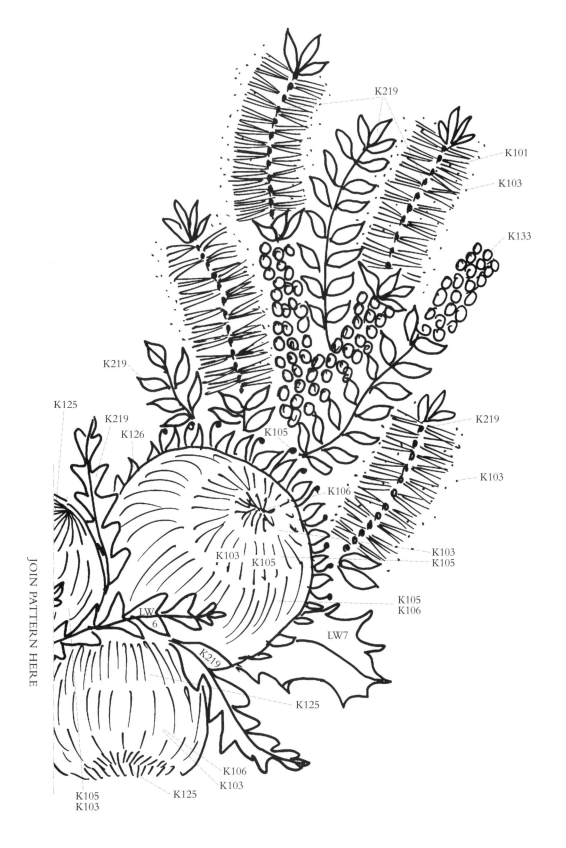

K219

K101

K103

K133

K219

K125

K219

K126

K105

K106

K219

K103

K103
K105

JOIN PATTERN HERE

K103   K105

LW 6

LW7

K219

K105
K106

K105
K125

K125

K106
K103

K105
K103

Blanket

THREADS	NUMBERS	THREADS	NUMBERS
KIRRA 2 PLY	308 x 2	KIRRA 2 PLY	232 x 1
KIRRA 2 PLY	305 x 2	KIRRA 2 PLY	413 x 2
KIRRA 2 PLY	303 x 2	KIRRA 2 PLY	414 x 2
KIRRA 2 PLY	302 x 2	KIRRA 2 PLY	419 x 3
KIRRA 2 PLY	401 x 1	KIRRA 2 PLY	105 x 1
KIRRA 2 PLY	402 x 1	KIRRA 2 PLY	114 x 1
KIRRA 2 PLY	403 x 1	LITTLEWOOD	7 x 1

Blanket

METHOD

The blanket in this book has been worked in 2 strands of 2 ply wool. You may use Kirra 4 ply for a similar look. It is however necessary to use 2 ply when using two colours in the needle.

1. Mark the pattern onto the blanket. Fold the blanket into four and mark the centre with a washable pencil. Centre the wreath around the centre mark and transfer the pattern (see page 4). Mark the centre direction line of each spray with running stitch and mark in the centre of the daisies with a colonial knot. It is not necessary to mark in the petals of the daisies when tracing the design. The small daisy sprays are marked randomly over the blanket.

2. To embroider the daisies follow the colour guide and flower glossary. Work feather stitch sprays between the flowers. Place fly stitches around the buds.

The small daisy sprays are placed and coloured randomly.

CONSTRUCTION OF BLANKET

1. Lightly press the finished work from the back.
2. Place the cotton backing material into place, edge to edge and tack into place.
3. Place the binding over the edges turning in the raw ends and mitring the corners.
4. Use a large zig zag stitch to sew into place.

FLOWERS

Daisies

STITCHES

Straight Stitch
Feather Stitch
Fly Stitch

MATERIALS

cream blanketing,
1.1 m x 1.1 m
(1 yard x 1 yard)

cotton lining,
1.1 m x 1.1 m
(1 yard x 1 yard)

blanket edging,
4.6 m (5 yards)
of blanket edging

washout pen

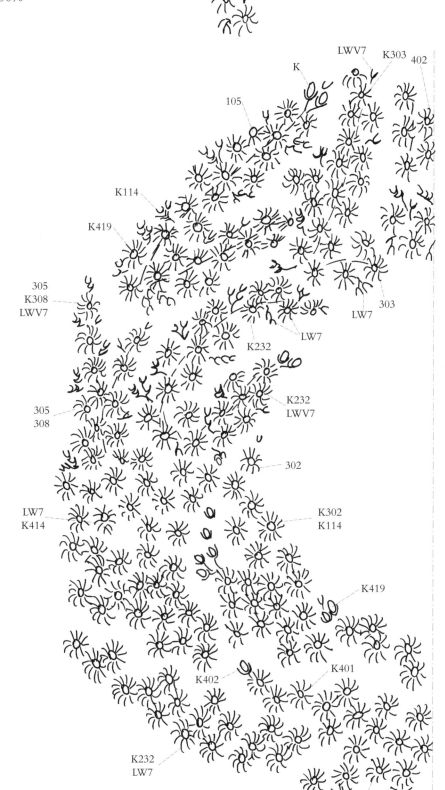

K

LWV7   K303   402

105

K114

K419

305
K308
LWV7

303

LW7

LW7

K232

K232
LWV7

305
308

302

LW7
K414

K302
K114

K419

K401

K402

JOIN TWO HALVES OF PATTERN HERE

K232
LW7

402

401
LW7

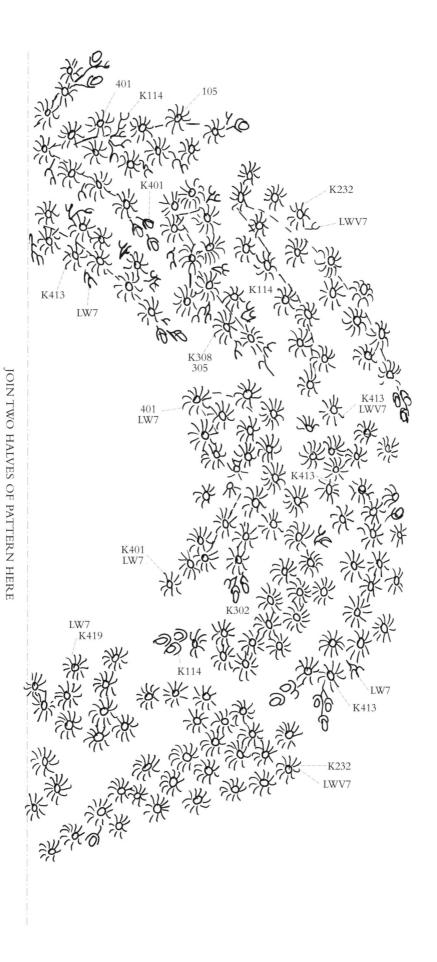

401
K114
105
K401
K232
LWV7
K413
LW7
K114
K308
305
K413
LWV7
401
LW7
K413
K401
LW7
K302
LW7
K419
K114
LW7
K413
K232
LWV7

JOIN TWO HALVES OF PATTERN HERE

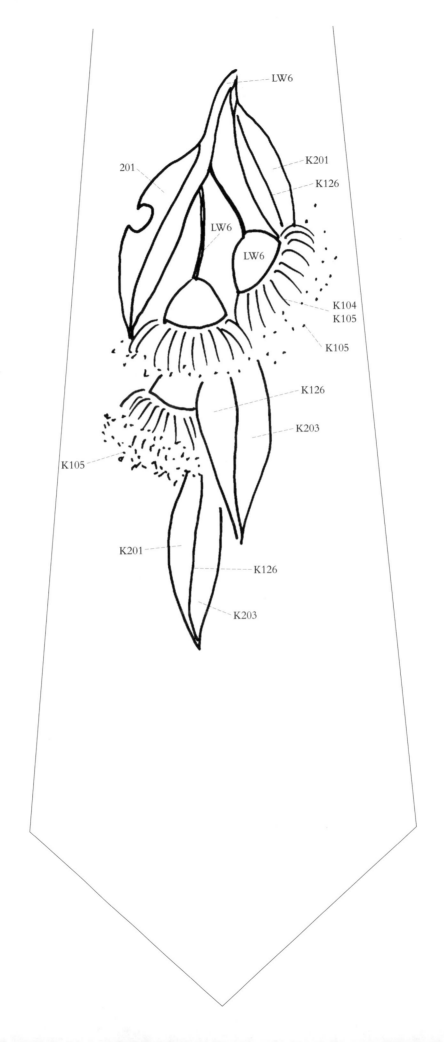

Tie

METHOD

1. Unpick the centre seam at the back of the tie from the wide end for approximately 35 cm (14").
2. Transfer the design onto the front of the tie.
3. Embroider the design following the flower glossary and colour guide.
4. Steam press the finished work. Slip stitch the back opening closed.

THREADS	NUMBERS
Leaves	
KIRRA 2PLY	201 x 1
	203 x 1
Veins	
KIRRA 2PLY	126 x 1
Stamens	
KIRRA 2PLY	104 x 1
Stamens and pollen	
KIRRA 2PLY	105 x 1
Stems, calyx	
LITTLEWOOD 2PLY	6 x 1

FLOWERS

Eucalyptus

MATERIALS

purchased wool tie

Cream Eucalypt Flower and Leaves Vest

THREADS	NUMBERS	THREADS	NUMBERS
KIRRA WOOL 2PLY	101 x 1	KIRRA WOOL 2PLY	210 x 2
	103 x 3		213 x 1
	105 x 3		214 x 1
	106 x 1		230 x 2
	125 x 2		231 x 2
	126 x 2		232 x 3
	128 x 1		233 x 3
	133 x 1		330 x 1
			331 x 1

Cream Eucalypt Flower and Leaves Vest

METHOD

1. Cut out two vest fronts from the pattern (see page 97). Zig zag around the edges with a sewing machine to prevent fraying. Stay stitch along front edges to prevent stretching.

2. Transfer the design onto the vest fronts. Refer to transfer instructions on page 4.

3. Work the embroidery following the directions in the Stitch and Flower Glossaries. Refer to methods detailed in Working with Wool. Follow the stitch and colour guide on the printed pattern.

4. When your embroidery is finished trim any long tails from the back. Check carefully that all the leaves are filled in and that all the veins and details are in place.

5. Steam press into shape. Leave to cool and dry completely.

Note: When embroidering a large design I steam and press it lightly several times while working on it. This prevents puckers and helps keep the work in shape.

CONSTRUCTION OF VEST

Vest designs may be used in conjunction with purchased vest patterns. Use your favourite pattern. Most importantly make sure it fits you. Remember that fabric on which you complete embroidery will 'shrink'.

1. Cut the lining for the vest using the embroidered fronts as your pattern. Cut two fronts and one back. Cut one back from wool flannel.

2. Sew shoulder seams.

3. Place lining and the wool vest with right sides together. Tack around the armholes. Tack around the fronts of the vest, from points A to B.

4. Sew and clip curves

5. Turn to the right side by pulling the fronts through the shoulder seams towards the back.

6. Press.

7. Sew the underarm seams and press flat.

8. Turn the lower edge to the inside and sew from the points on the front of the vest past the side seams into the back. Sew from the point towards the back on either side leaving an opening at the centre back.

9. Clip the points and turn to the right side. Press and close the back opening by hand with a small slip stitch.

PATTERN SIZE

Medium

FLOWERS

Eucalypt

STITCHES

Stem Stitch
Straight Stitch
Buttonhole Wheels
Colonial Knot
Turkey Stitch

MATERIALS

Kirra hand-dyed wool flannel, 80 cm x 115 cm (32" x 46")
lining fabric, 80 cm x 115 cm (32" x 46")
embroidery scissors
dressmaking scissors
crewel needles, size 5
washout fabric marker
tracing paper

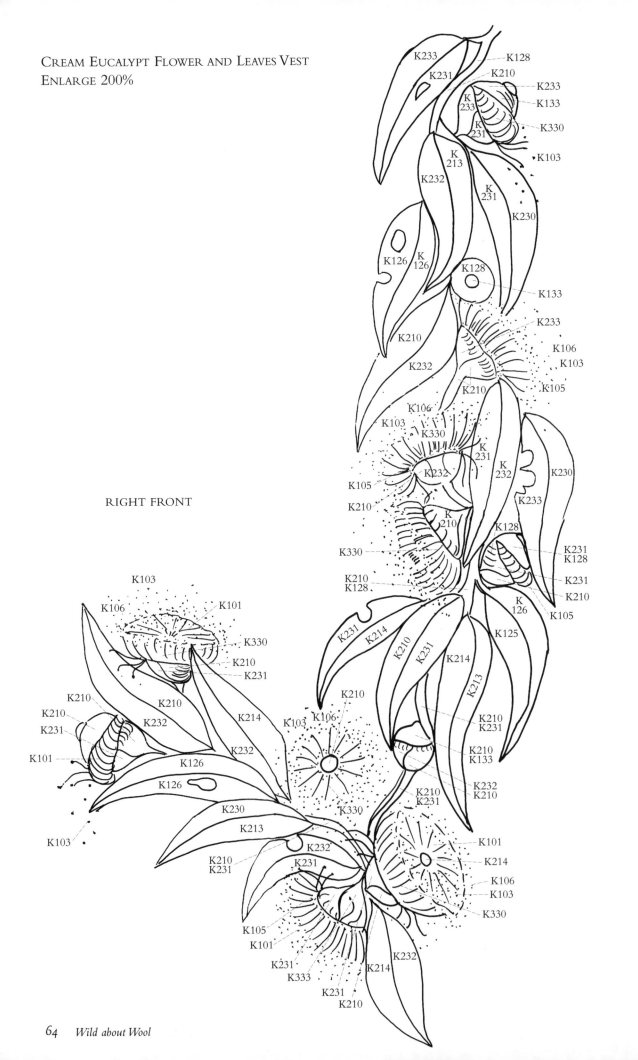

CREAM EUCALYPT FLOWER AND LEAVES VEST
ENLARGE 200%

RIGHT FRONT

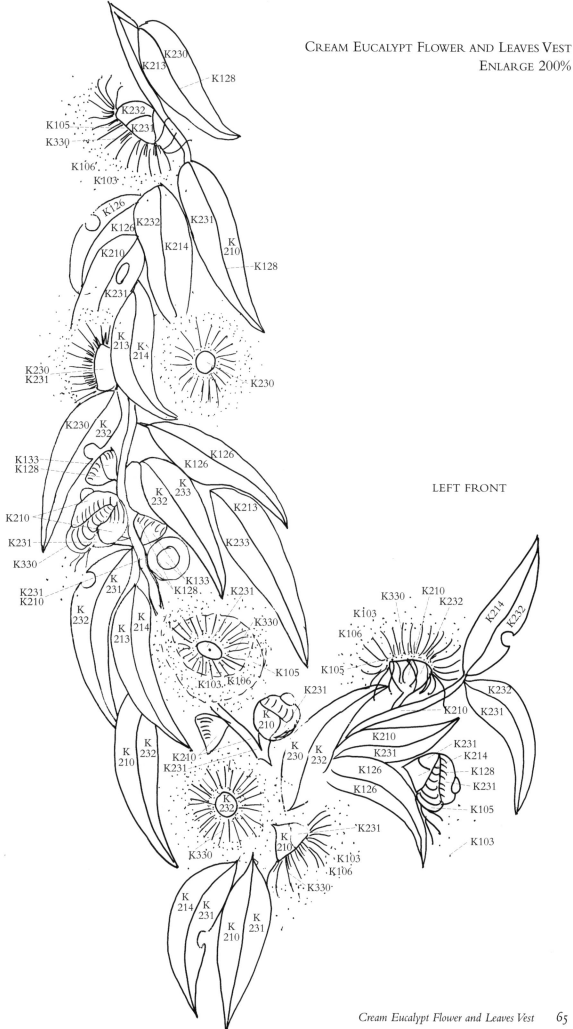

LEFT FRONT

Honey Eaters Vest

THREADS	NUMBERS	THREADS	NUMBERS
BIRDS		**LEAVES**	
KIRRA 2PLY	104 x 1	KIRRA 2PLY	113 x 2
	133 x 1		114 x 2
LITTLEWOOD	1000 x 1		117 x 1
	70 x 1		126 x 2
	630 x 1		204 x 2
	615 x 1		205 x 2
			207 x 2
			208 x 2
FLOWERS			
KIRRA 2 PLY	103 x 2	**VEINS**	
	204 x 2		
	330 x 5	KIRRA 2PLY	126 x1
			128 x1

Honey Eaters Vest

New Holland Honey Eaters are common throughout southern and eastern Australia as far north as Brisbane. They are extremely noisy assertive birds and congregate in great numbers in nectar-bearing native plants. Each evening in the summer dozens of them arrive in the shrubs in my garden waiting for the water sprinklers to be turned on.

Method

Follow steps 1–5 given on page 63.

Embroidery Instructions

1. Work the stems and flower centres first then add the stamens and pollen dots. Refer to Flower Glossary on page 13.

2. The Honey Eater birds are worked in stem stitch and straight stitch. Feather the areas where the colour blends from black to white with short straight stitches. The predominantly black areas on the back and wings are blended with some grey and yellow stitches. The stitches are worked from the head through to the tail. The legs are worked in stem stitch, the eye, one colonial knot. Follow the stitch and colour guide for birds and leaves on the printed pattern.

To make up the vest refer to construction methods detailed on page 63.

Pattern Size

Medium

Flowers

Eucalypt

Stitches

Stem Stitch
Straight Stitch
Colonial Knot
Buttonhole Wheels
Bullion Stitch

Materials

wool flannel,
80 cm x 115 cm
(32" x 46")
acetate lining,
80 cm x 115 cm
(32" x 46")
embroidery hoop
12.5 cm (5")
crewel needles, size 5
commercial vest pattern

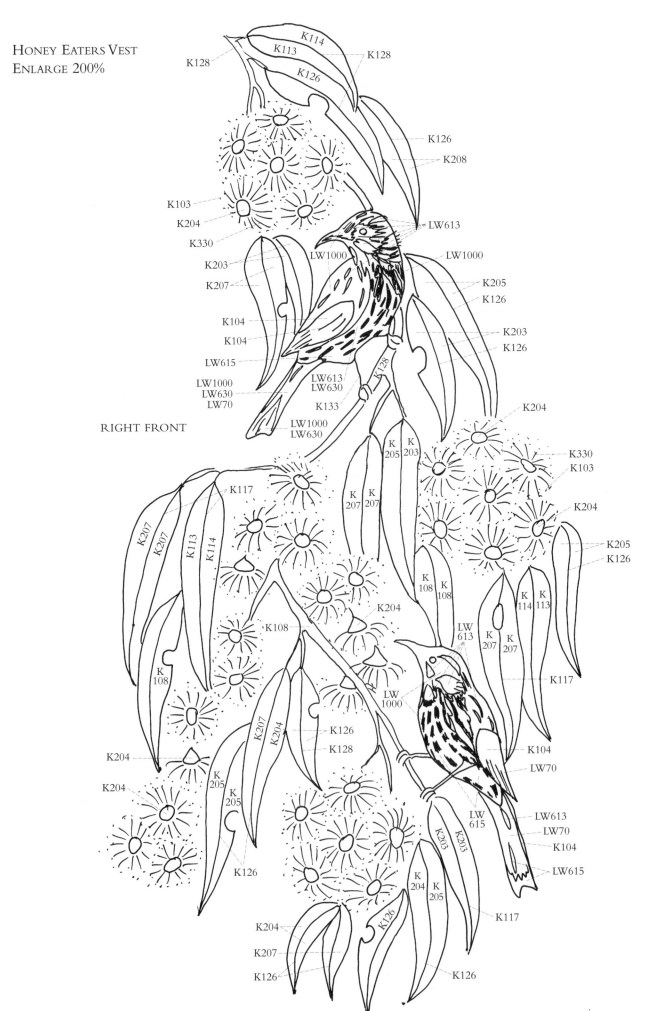

HONEY EATERS VEST
ENLARGE 200%

K128

K114
K113
K126
K128

K126
K208

K103
K204
K330

LW613

K203
K207

LW1000

LW1000

K205
K126

K104
K104

K203
K126

LW615

LW1000
LW630
LW70

LW613
LW630

K128

K133

LW1000
LW630

K205 K203

K204

K330
K103

K204

K205
K126

RIGHT FRONT

K117

K207
K207
K113
K114

K207
K207

K108
K108

K114 K113

K108

LW
613

K207
K207

K
108

K204

K117

LW
1000

K126
K128

K104

K207
K204

LW70

K204

K205
K205

LW
615

LW613
LW70
K104

K203
K203

LW615

K117

K126

K204
K205

K126

K204
K207
K126

K126

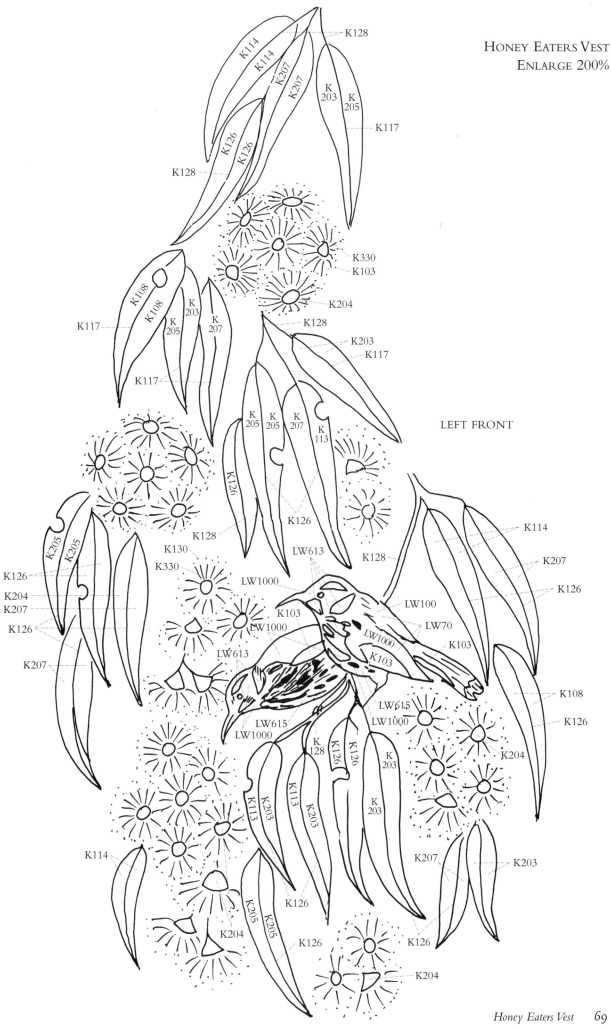

LEFT FRONT

Australian Floral Emblem Vest

THREADS	NUMBERS	THREADS	NUMBERS
BLUE GUM		**PINK HEATH**	
Leaves and stems		*Stems and leaves*	
KIRRA 2PLY	223 x 1	KIRRA 2PLY	207 x 1
	225 x 1	*Trumpets*	
	226 x 1	KIRRA 2PLY	307 x 1
			304 x 1
FLOWER AND BUD		*Stars*	
Centre		KIRRA 2PLY	330 x 1
KIRRA 2PLY	216 x 1	**STURTS DESERT ROSE**	
Stamens and pollen	*101 x 1*	*Petals*	
Pollen	105 x 1	KIRRA 2PLY	302 x 1
			303 x 1
STURT DESERT PEA			304 x 1
Petals		APPLETON	145 x 1
APPLETONS	502 x 1	*Leaves*	
	995 x 1	KIRRA 2PLY	215 x 1
LITTLEWOOD	681 x 1		216 x 1
	613 x 1	*Veins*	
Centre		KIRRA 2PLY	223 x 1
LITTLEWOOD	1000 x 1	*Stamens*	
Leaves		KIRRA 2PLY	331 x 1
KIRRA 2PLY	232 x 1		
		WARATAH	
COOKTOWN ORCHIDS		*Petals*	
Petals		LITTLEWOOD	681 x 1
KIRRA 2PLY	303 x 1	APPLETON	145 x 1
	304 x 1		502 x 1
Stems and leaves		*Highlights*	
KIRRA 2PLY	215 x 1	KIRRA 2PLY	306 x 1
Centre		*Leaves*	
APPLETON	145 x 1	KIRRA 2PLY	215 x 1
		Veins	
WATTLE—VERSION 3		KIRRA 2PLY	223 x 1
Stems and leaves			
KIRRA 2PLY	211 x 1	**BLUEBELL**	
Flowers		*Petal*	
KIRRA 2PLY	104	APPLETON	740 x 1
		Shading	
KANGAROO PAW		DMC BM	6688 x 1
Flower		*Centre*	
KIRRA 2PLY	220 x 1	LITTLEWOOD	613 x 1
	218 x 1	*Leaves and stems*	
Stamens and turn-backs		KIRRA 2PLY	214 x 1
KIRRA 2PLY	224 x 1		
Stems			
LITTLEWOOD	681 x 1		

Australian Floral Emblem Vest

THE ORIGINAL PATTERN OF THIS VEST WAS DESIGNED FOR A SMALL SIZE, HOWEVER,
THE DESIGN WOULD LOOK EQUALLY AT HOME ON A MEDIUM SIZE. CENTRE THE DESIGN TO THE VEST FRONT
PATTERN BEFORE TRANSFERRING USING THE TRACING PAPER METHOD. SINGLE FLOWER ELEMENTS CAN BE USED ON
ANY OTHER PROJECT YOU HAVE IN MIND—A MATCHING BERET OR BAG PERHAPS?

METHOD

This pattern is designed for a small vest. If you wish to make a larger garment I would suggest marking the sprays of flowers on the material separately and placing them further apart—thus increasing the overall size of the design. Remember, you can always fill gaps in the design with extra leaves, buds or small sprays of wattle.

Follow steps 1–5 given on page 63.

Make up vest according to instructions on page 63.

PATTERN SIZE:

Small / Medium

FLOWERS

*Tasmanian Blue
Gum–Eucalypt
Sturt Desert Pea
Cooktown Orchid
Wattle–Version 3
Kangaroo Paw
Pink Heath
Sturts Desert Rose
Waratah
Bluebell*

STITCHES

*Buttonhole Stars
Stem Stitch
Fly Stitch
Pistil Stitch
Colonial Knots
Detached Chain Stitch*

MATERIALS

*black wool
flannel–according to
size on pattern
black noire taffeta
for lining
scissors
embroidery hoop, 5"
crewel needle, size 5
tracing paper
commercial vest pattern*

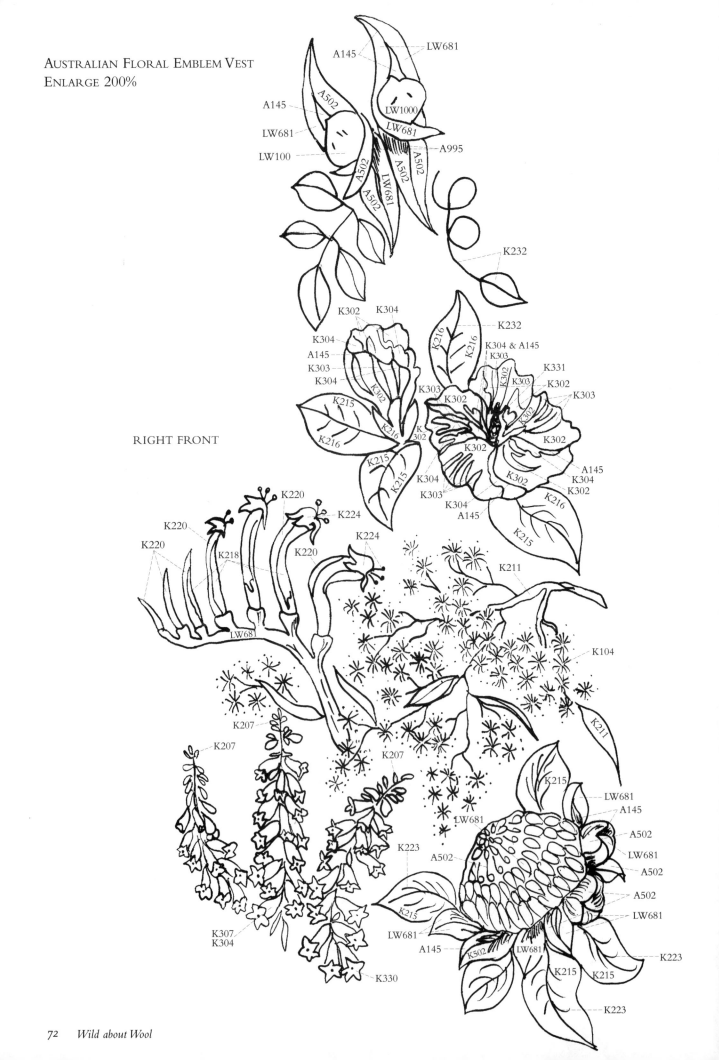

AUSTRALIAN FLORAL EMBLEM VEST
ENLARGE 200%

A145   LW681

A145

A502

LW681

LW100

A502

LW1000

LW681

A995

A502

A502

LW681

A502

A502

K232

K302   K304

K304

A145

K303

K304

K215

K216

K215

K215

K216

K216

K302

K216

K302

K303

K302

K303

K304 & A145

K303

K331

K302

K303

K302

K302

K302

K302

K302

K302

K302

A145

K304

K302

K216

K215

K304

K303

K304

A145

RIGHT FRONT

K220

K220

K224

K220

K218

K220

K224

K211

K104

LW681

K207

K207

K207

K223

K211

K215

LW681

A145

A502

LW681

A502

A502

LW681

LW681

A502

A145

K502

LW681

K223

K307
K304

K330

K215

LW681

K215   K215

K223

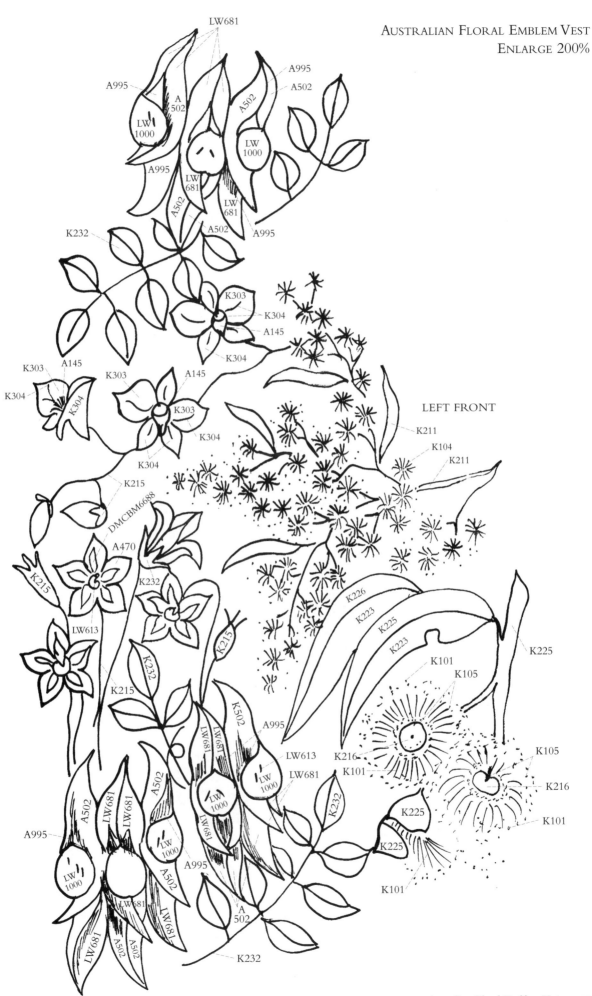

LEFT FRONT

Western Spinebills Vest

THREADS	NUMBERS	THREADS	NUMBERS
BOTTLEBRUSH		BIRDS	
Leaves		KIRRA 2 PLY	131 x 1
KIRRA 2 PLY	203 x 1		132 x 1
	207 x 1		134 x 1
			330 x 1
Stems			322 x 1
KIRRA 2 PLY	211 x 1		333 x 1
Flowers		LITTLEWOOD	1000 x 1
KIRRA 2 PLY	101 x 2		
	102 x 2		
	115 x 2		
Pollen			
KIRRA 2 PLY	101 x 1		
Seed pods			
KIRRA 2 PLY	127 x 1		
	128 x 1		

Western Spinebills Vest

THIS DESIGN WOULD SUIT ALMOST ANY SIZE VEST, WITH MINOR ADJUSTMENTS.

METHOD

Follow steps 1–5 given on page 63.

EMBROIDERY INSTRUCTIONS

1. Follow directions in flower glossary for bottlebrush flowers and seed pods.
2. Work the leaves and stems in stem stitch.
3. Scatter some of the gold seed beads among the pollen to catch the light.
4. The birds are worked in rows of stem stitch. Blend the grey to create lines of colour along the tail and wing areas.
5. Work a narrow line of black along the centre of the bills and work the eye in black in a colonial knot.
6. Work the legs in stem stitch and the claws in bullion stitch with 11–16 wraps and couch into a curved shape with a small stitch.

Make up vest according to instructions given on page 63.

FLOWERS

Bottlebrush Flowers and Seed Pods

STITCHES

Stem Stitch
Colonial Knot
Bullion Stitch and Circle
Stem Stitch

MATERIALS

terracotta wool blend—
according to pattern size
olive green taffeta lining—
according to pattern size
small gold seed beads
scissors
embroidery hoop, 5"
crewel needle, size 5
tracing paper
commercial vest pattern

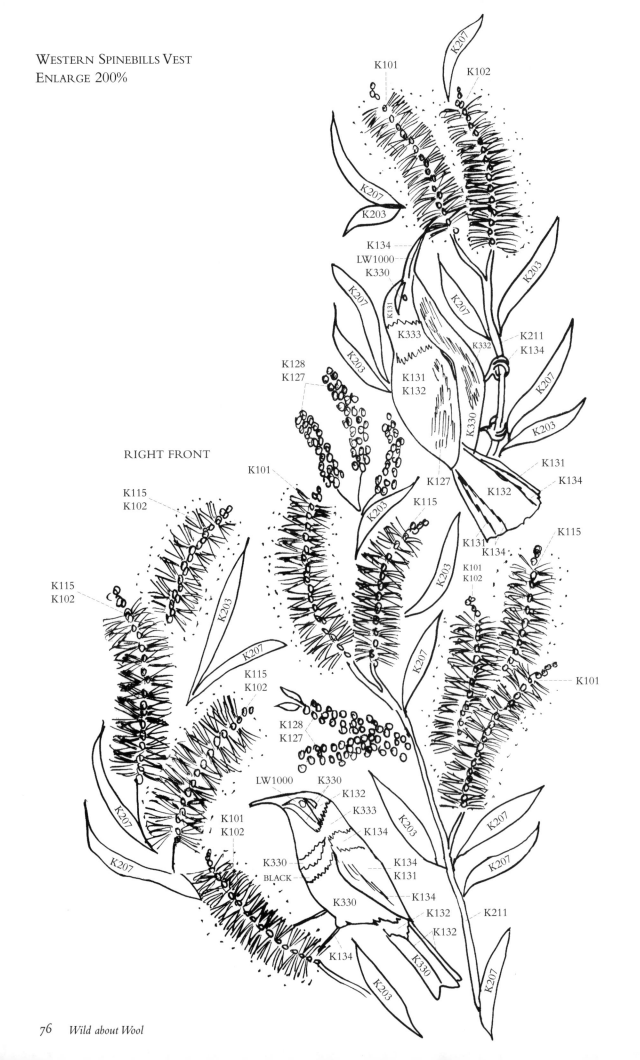

RIGHT FRONT

K203
K203
K203
K115
K101
K134
K132
K132
K330
K134
K132
K207
K211
K131
K330
K330
K134
K128
K127
K330
LW1000
K330
K333
K203
K132
K207
K115
K203
LEFT FRONT
K330
K132
K203
K203
K207
K203
K102
K101
K102
K203
K207
K207
K211
K101
K115
K115
K115
K102
K128
K127
K115
K101
K203
K330 LW1000 K134
K131
K207
K333
K131
K132
K330
K127
K134
K207
K211
K207 K207 K203 K203 K207 K211
K115
K134
K132
K131

Red Eucalypt Vest

THREADS	NUMBERS	THREADS	NUMBERS
FLOWERS		FLOWERS	
Stamens		*Veins*	
LITTLEWOOD	681 x 1	KIRRA 2PLY	221 x 1
APPLETONS	502 x 1	*Gumnuts*	
Pollen		KIRRA 2PLY	128 x 1
KIRRA 2PLY	103 x 4		127 x 1
Leaves and stems			116 x 1
KIRRA 2PLY	225 x 2		
	228 x 2	*'Holes'*	
	216 x 2	KIRRA 2 PLY	122 x 1
	214 x 2		
	217 x 1		
	223 x 2		
	222 x 2		

Red Eucalypt Vest
Eucalyptus Macrocarpa

THE RED EUCALYPT IS A SMALL MALLEE TREE WITH A STRAGGLING CROWN OF SILVER GREY FOLIAGE. THE FLOWERS ARE LARGE AND RED, OCCASIONALLY PINK, COMPRISING MANY STAMENS AROUND A CENTRAL DISC. IT FLOWERS MAINLY IN WINTER AND IS NATIVE TO SOUTH-WEST WESTERN AUSTRALIA AND IS WIDELY CULTIVATED AS A GARDEN TREE.

METHOD

The vest pictured is a medium size but the design would fit a size larger or smaller.

Follow steps 1–5 given on page 63.

EMBROIDERY INSTRUCTIONS

Work all flowers and leaves following Eucalypt directions in the flower glossary. The veins on the leaves and some edges around the gumnuts are worked in stem stitch after all other embroidery is finished. Work around the holes and chewed edges of the leaves in stem stitch.

When working the flowers work the stamens and small red centres first and pack the colonial knots 'pollen' close together using the coloured picture as a guide.

Make up vest according to instructions given on page 63.

PATTERN SIZE

Medium

FLOWERS

Eucalypt

STITCHES

Stem Stitch
Straight Stitch
Buttonhole Stitch
Colonial Knot
Uncut Turkey Stitch

MATERIALS

purchased vest pattern
wool flannel as recommended in pattern—dark grey or black
lining fabric—red moire taffeta or silk
dressmakers scissors
sharp embroidery scissors
crewel needle, size 5
tailors chalk
tracing paper

RED EUCALYPT VEST
ENLARGE 200%

K216
K222   K214
K217   K222
        A502
K228
        K216
        K116
K223   K222
K216   K225
LW681   K225   K128
        K116
        K233
K222 K228 K223
            K216
            K222
K223   K214
K216   K222
K225
K228   K223   LW681
K222   K222
    LW681   K228
                        K103
LW681
A502   K223   K222
K214   K223
K216   K216
K216   K116
K223   K222
K217   A502
K216   K222   LW681
        K224
        K223
        K223
K223   K228
        K223
        K216
RIGHT FRONT
K223   K228
K216   K222
K223   K225
K222
K223
K222   LW681
K217
K214   LW681
K228   K216   K225
K222   K214   K216   K103
A502   K223   LW681
K103   K217   K216
K127   K216   K222   K216
K116   K223   K216
K214   K228   K214   K225
K223   K225
        K222   K216
        K228   A502
        K225
A502

80   Wild about Wool

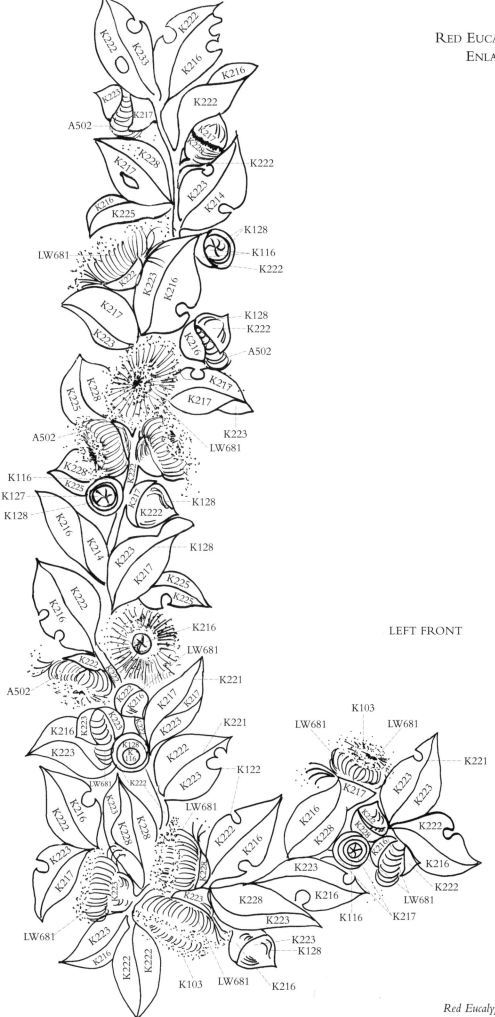

LEFT FRONT

Tea Tree and Blue Wren Vest

THREADS	NUMBERS	THREADS	NUMBERS
TEA TREE		BIRDS	
Petals		*Chest*	
KIRRA 2PLY	330 x 4	KIRRA 2 PLY	331 x 1
	305 x 1	LITTLEWOOD	259 x 1
	307 x 1	*Wing*	
	202, 216 x 1	KIRRA 2 PLY	128 x 1
	201 x 1	*Head and face*	
APPLETONS	995 x 1	APPLETON	462 x 1
Stems		*Tail*	
KIRRA 2 PLY	130 x 1	KIRRA 2 PLY	429 x 1
Leaves		*Leg*	
KIRRA 2 PLY	216 x 2	KIRRA 2 PLY	133 x 1
	214 x 2	*Back*	
	232 x 2	LITTLEWOOD	1000 x 1

Tea Tree and Blue Wren Vest

THIS PATTERN HAS BEEN DESIGNED TO FIT THE FRONTS OF A MEDIUM SIZED VEST. TO FIT A SMALLER SIZE IT MAY BE NECESSARY TO OMIT A FEW FLOWERS AND LEAVES AT EACH END OF THE DESIGN. FOR A LARGER DESIGN CONTINUE THE LEAVES AND FLOWERS ON AT EACH END OF THE PATTERN.

METHOD

Follow steps 1–5 given on page 63.

Note: Use tracing paper method when transferring this design onto vest front. Mark in design line stems as on pattern. Mark the birds in detail. Mark in only the centres of the main groups of flowers.

EMBROIDERY INSTRUCTIONS

1. Work stems first in stem stitch.

2. Work the flowers up and over the stems and add leaves to fill in open areas of all. Work most of the flowers in cream and scatter some in pink amongst the cream. Add two or three deep red straight stitches around most of the centres and scatter stamens randomly on some of the petals.

3. The leaves are worked randomly in the three colours recommended. Use the colour picture as a guide only and as long as the stems are mostly covered in flowers and leaves the design will look good.

4. Follow directions for working bird in Blue Wren Cushion.

Make up vest according to instructions given on page 63.

BIRDS

Blue Wrens—Male

FLOWERS

Tea Tree

STITCHES

Buttonhole Wheels
Stem Stitch
Straight Stitch
Colonial Knots

MATERIALS

purchased vest pattern
dark grey wool flannel as recommended on pattern
lining fabric, deep red moire taffeta
scissors, dressmaking, embroidery
crewel needle, size 5
tailors chalk or washout fabric marker
tracing paper

TEA TREE AND BLUE WREN VEST
ENLARGE 200%

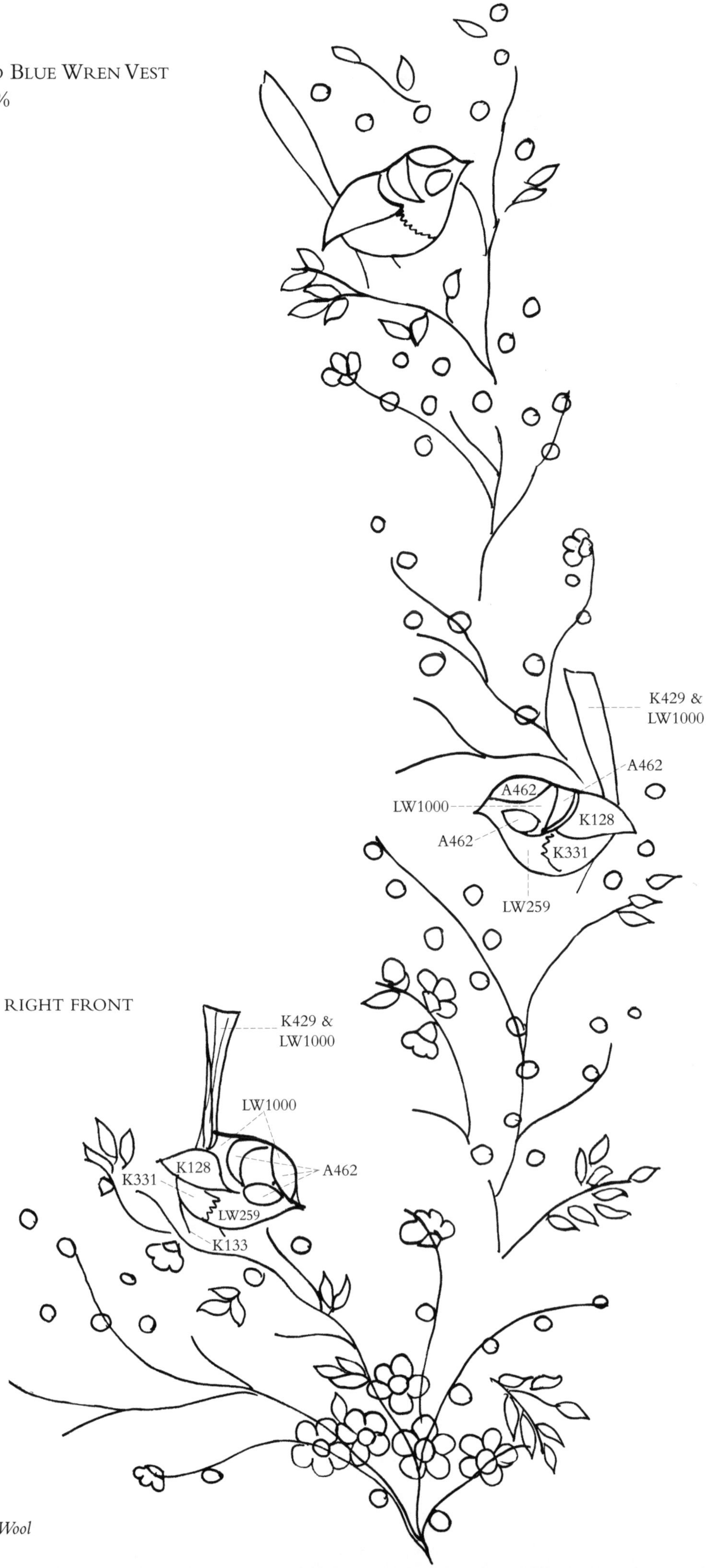

K429 &
LW1000

A462

LW1000

A462

A462

K128

K331

LW259

RIGHT FRONT

K429 &
LW1000

LW1000

K128

A462

K331

LW259

K133

LEFT FRONT

K429
LW1000

LW1000

LW613

A462

A462

LW
259

A462

K128

K331

K133

K130

K202
or K216

K330

Flower petals
K330 or K305

'Purple Hills' Wildflower Vest

THIS VEST WAS DESIGNED FOR MY OWN ENJOYMENT AND I NEVER EXPECTED TO HAVE TO MAKE A PATTERN FOR IT OR TO COME UP WITH 'HOW TO' INSTRUCTIONS. I WOULD SUGGEST THAT IF YOU WISH TO MAKE THIS GARMENT YOU HAVE AS MUCH FUN AS I DID AND USE THE PATTERN AS A GUIDE ONLY. YOU MAY WISH TO SUBSTITUTE SOME FLOWERS OR CHANGE THE COLOURS OF OTHERS.

MATERIALS

It is difficult to give exact measurements for fabric for this vest. Be guided by a purchased pattern. Divide the two main colours roughly in half. You only need a small piece, approximately 28 cms (11-12") across in the purple. It may be difficult to find wool flannel in these colours. A wool blend would be a suitable alternative. You could even try linen.

Choose a lining colour to match one of the main colour fabrics so as not to introduce any more colour. Choose a purple coloured wool to match the hills to use for the applique and for the lines on the hills.

METHOD

1. Trace off the patterns for the three different coloured background sections and cut out (see diagram below). Place the materials over the entire pattern for the vest to ensure correct alignment before basting into position.

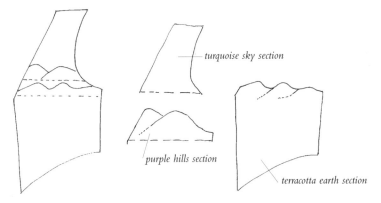

turquoise sky section

purple hills section

terracotta earth section

The broken line on the pattern just below the 'hill' line is the cutting line for the bottom of the sky and purple hills section. Cut the turquoise 'sky' to this line in the vest shape then cut out the purple hills tracing directly from the pattern. Place the purple hills over the turquoise and into position. Cut the 'earth' or terracotta section of the vest using your own vest pattern and tracing the 'hills' lines from the pattern in this book. Baste over the two other pieces of material.

FLOWERS

Hardenbergia
Fringed Lily
Eucalypts
Poached Egg Daisy
Flannel Flower
Golden Wattle
Sturt Desert Pea
Silver Wattle
Showy Groundsel
Blackboy
Bottlebrush
Parakeelya
Small Daisies
Blunts Everlasting
Kangaroo Apple
Sturts Desert Rose
Parrot Pea

STITCHES

Stem Stitch
Straight Stitch
Satin Stitch
Buttonhole
Colonial Knots
Fly Stitch

METHOD CONTINUED

2. When all pieces of material are joined together embroider over the joins using a purple wool thread and satin stitch for the purple hills and Kirra 223 for random rows of colonial knots for the lower hills. Vary the width of this line making sure to cover all raw edges. Work the lines on the purple hills in stem stitch through all layers of material. Work all the embroidery on this section through all layers of material and scatter random V shaped stitches over the earth coloured hills to anchor all layers of material together.

EMBROIDERY INSTRUCTIONS

1. Special note: When working a vest with the pattern all the way around, the construction of the garment is slightly different from others in this book. I joined the underarm seams first and worked from right to left around the vest.

2. Transfer the pattern onto the fabric marking in only the main guidelines and centres of flowers (see page 63). Use a chalk pencil to draw in the flower shapes freehand—its easy to rub away if you don't like the first attempt. When you are satisfied with your drawing run around the outline in small stitches before embroidering over it.

3. Follow the diagram and colour guide to complete all other embroidery, but remember to let your imagination go. Do not try and make the embroidery exactly as I have done.

Make up vest according to instructions given on page 63.

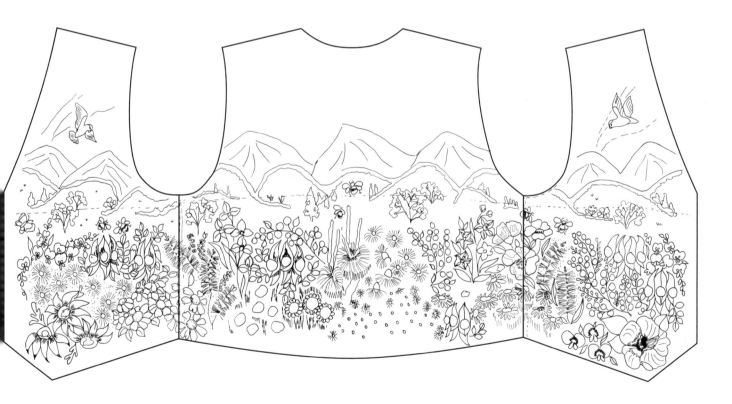

THREADS	NUMBERS	THREADS	NUMBERS

HARDENBERGIA

Upper petal
DMC BM — 8333 x 1
Lower petal
DMC BM — 8794 x 1
Green spots
DMC BM — 8421 x 1
Stems and leaves
KIRRA 2PLY — 218 x 1

LEMON EUCALYPTS

Centre
KIRRA 2PLY — 201 x 1
Stamens
KIRRA 2PLY — 101 x 1
KIRRA 2PLY — 102 x 1

Pollen
KIRRA 2PLY — 103 x 1

PINK EUCALYPT

Centre
KIRRA 2PLY — 201 x 1
Stamens
KIRRA 2PLY — 318 x 1
Pollen
KIRRA 2PLY — 330 x 1

FLANNEL FLOWER

Petal
KIRRA 2PLY — 330 x 1
Centre
KIRRA 2PLY — 223 x 1
KIRRA 2PLY — 226 x 1
KIRRA 2PLY — 221 x 1

Leaves
KIRRA 2PLY — 223 x 1

STURT DESERT PEA

Petals
APPLETON — 502 x 1
— 995 x 1
LITTLEWOOD — 681 x 1
Centre
LITTLEWOOD — 1000 x 1
or KIRRA 2PLY — BLACK x 1
White highlight
KIRRA 2PLY — 330 x 1
Leaves
KIRRA 2PLY — 232 x 1

SHOWY GROUNDSEL

Petals
KIRRA 2PLY — 120 x 1
Centre
KIRRA 2PLY — 130 x 1
Pollen
KIRRA 2PLY — 120 x 1
KIRRA 2PLY — 121 x 1

Leaves
KIRRA 2PLY — 219 x 1

APRICOT BOTTLEBRUSH

Centre line and leaves
KIRRA 2PLY — 218 x 1
Stamens
KIRRA 2PLY — 332 x 1
KIRRA 2PLY — 334 x 1

Pollen
KIRRA 2PLY — 330 x 1
Seed Cases
KIRRA 2PLY — 130 x 1

LEMON BOTTLEBRUSH

Centre line and leaves
KIRRA 2PLY — 218 x 1
Stamens
KIRRA 2PLY — 102 x 1
Pollen
KIRRA 2PLY — 104 x 1

THREADS	NUMBERS	THREADS	NUMBERS
FRINGED LILY		**KANGAROO APPLE**	
DMC BM	8331 x 1	*Petals*	
	8333 x 1	DMC BM	8332 x 1
Leaves			8332 x 1
KIRRA 2PLY	222 x 1	*Centre*	
Centre		KIRRA 2PLY	104 x 1
KIRRA 2PLY	104 x 1	*Leaves*	
		KIRRA 2PLY	232 x 1
POACHED EGG DAISY			
		SMALL DAISIES	
Centre			
KIRRA 2PLY	130 x 1	*Petals*	
Petals		KIRRA 2PLY	428 x 1
KIRRA 2PLY	330 x 1		427 x 1
Leaves			
KIRRA 2PLY	219 x 1	*Centre*	
		KIRRA 2PLY	104 x 1
		Leaves	
GOLDEN WATTLE		KIRRA 2PLY	218 x 1
Stems			
KIRRA 2PLY	128 x 1	**BLUNT EVERLASTING**	
Leaves			
KIRRA 2PLY	218 x 1	*Petals*	
Flowers		KIRRA 2PLY	330 x 1
KIRRA 2PLY	104 x 1	*Centre*	
		KIRRA 2PLY	102 x 1
		Leaves	
SILVER WATTLE		KIRRA 2PLY	201 x 1
Stems			
KIRRA 2PLY	223 x 1	**PARAKEELYA**	
Leaves			
KIRRA 2PLY	223 x 1	*Petals*	
Flowers		KIRRA 2PLY	314 x 1
KIRRA 2PLY	102 x 1		311 x 1
		Centre	
BLACKBOY		KIRRA 2PLY	104 x 1
			330 x 1
Stems		*Leaves*	
KIRRA 2PLY	128 x 1	KIRRA 2PLY	201 x 1
	127 x 1		
		PARROT PEA	
Leaves			
KIRRA 2PLY	218 x 1	*Large petals*	
	221 x 1	KIRRA 2PLY	120 x 1
	220 x 1	*Centre*	
	128 x 1	KIRRA 2PLY	102 x 1
	127 x 1	*Highlight and lower petal*	
Flowers		APPLETON	502 x 1
DMC BM	8421 x 1		

THREADS	NUMBERS
DESERT ROSE	
Petals	
KIRRA 2PLY	302 x 1
	304 x 1
	303 x 1
APPLETON	145 x 1
Stamens	
KIRRA 2PLY	330 x 1
Leaves	
KIRRA 2PLY	216 x 1

COLONIAL KNOT 'BUSHES' EDGE TO HILLS AND SMALL MALLEE TREE	
KIRRA 2PLY	223 x 1
Stems	
KIRRA 2PLY	127 x 1

BEES	
Body	
KIRRA 2PLY	128 x 1
	104 x 1
Wings	
KIRRA 2PLY	330 x 1
Legs	
KIRRA 2PLY	128 x 1

THREADS	NUMBERS
BUTTERFLY	
KIRRA 2PLY	128 x 1
	312 x 1
LITTLEWOOD	1000 x 1

PINE TREES	
KIRRA 2PLY	221 x 1

GALAH	
Wings and tail	
KIRRA 2PLY	433 x 1
	431 x 1
Chest	
KIRRA	
	308 x 1

K330

K301

K308

LEFT FRONT

K223

K221 K221

K223

K223

K223 K223

K223

K312

K128

LW000

K127

K223

K330

K128

K104

K218

DMC
BM 8421

K218

DMC
BM 8333

DMC
BM 8794

LW681 A502 A502 A502

A502

K232

A502 A502

LW681

LW681

K332

A502

LW1000

LW1000

K330

A502

LW681 LW681

LW681

A502

K201

A995

A502

LW681

LW681

A502

K120

K130

K219

BM
8333

K102

K201

K101

K201

K130

K103

K330

K226 K223

K101

K201

K130

K120

K223 K226

K226 K223

K219 K120

K221

K221 K330

K120
K211

JOIN LEFT FRONT TO LEFT BACK

K223

PURPLE HILLS WILDFLOWER VEST
ENLARGE 200%

JOIN CENTRE BACK PATTERN HERE

RIGHT BACK

JOIN CENTRE BACK PATTERN HERE

K223

K223

K221

K221

K223

DMC
BM8421

K221

K318

K232

BM8332

K104

K311

K314

K218

K330

DMC
BM8333

K201

K201

K104

K314

K311

K201

K221

K201

K232

K218
K220

K314

K201

K128
K127

K104

K128

K218

K102

K102

K428

K427

K104

K104

K428
OR
K427

PURPLE HILLS WILDFLOWER VEST
ENLARGE 200%

H31
K433
K433

K302
K308

RIGHT FRONT

K221
K221
K221

JOIN RIGHT FRONT TO RIGHT BACK

K223
K223

K104
K330

DMC
BM8333
DMC
BM8421
DMC
BM8794

A995
A502   LW681
K223

LW1000

A502
A502
LW681

K201   K218

K102

DMC
BM8333

K218

K104

A502
A502

LW681

K102

K218

A502

LW681

A502
A502

K102

K223

LW681
A502
A995
A502

K218

K102

K218

K223

LW1000

A502
LW681
LW681
LW681

K223

K216

K102

K216

K216

K102

K303

K330

K102

K216

K302

K302

K120

K102

K304

A502
K102

K120

A502

K330

A995

94   Wild about Wool

Acknowledgments

Writing, researching, stitching the projects and collating the material for this book has been a much larger task than I first envisaged. When Cheryl Riste first suggested I undertake this task I thought 'Why not? No trouble!' I stand corrected! However the task has been made a lot easier by the encouragement and support of friends and family.

I would like to thank Colleen Murtagh for her help in putting together my random thoughts in the text of the introduction. Ruth Trigg for her encouragement and help in setting out the 'bones' of the book. My niece Samantha Bierbaum for her help in coping with the dreaded computer. My dear friends Judith and Margo for their unfailing encouragement and support at our weekly embroidery evenings. A special thanks to Cheryl Riste for her faith in this project and for unravelling my first handwritten draft. To Karen Bradford of Kayinga Silks for supplying the hand-painted woollen tie. I wish to thank Kirra Yarns for the donation of threads and hand-dyed wool flannel.

Last but not least my husband Joe who has picked up after me for 25 years.

Suppliers

RISTAL THREADS

Kirra Yarns/Wool Flannel
PO Box 134
Mitchell ACT 2911
Australia
Ph: (06) 241 2293
Fax: (06) 241 8382

STADIA HANDCRAFTS

Appletons Yarns
PO Box 495
Paddington NSW 2021
Australia
Ph: (02) 9328 7900
Fax: (02) 9326 1768

LITTLEWOOD FLEECE YARNS

46 Tarcombe Street
Euroa VIC 3666
Australia
Ph: (03) 579 0234

Vest Pattern

ENLARGE 400%

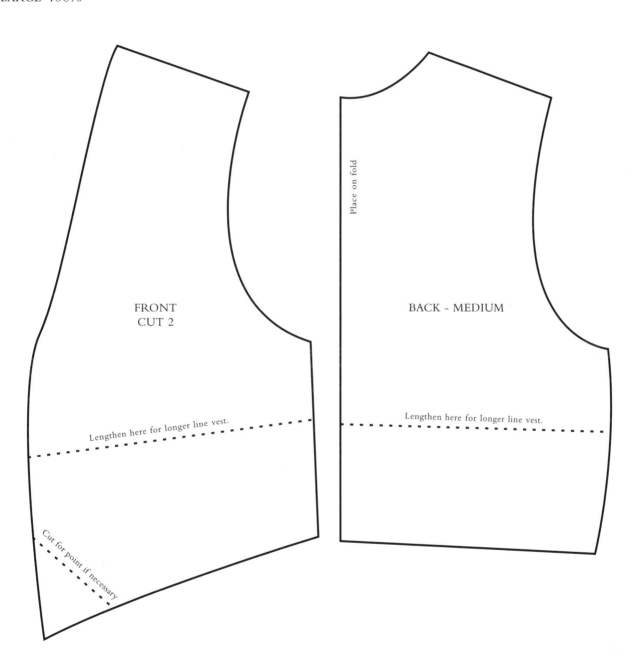

FRONT
CUT 2

Lengthen here for longer line vest.

Cut for point if necessary

Place on fold

BACK - MEDIUM

Lengthen here for longer line vest.

Thread Conversion Chart

KIRRA	APPLETONS 2 PLY	BRODER MEDICI DMC	KIRRA	APPLETONS 2 PLY	BRODER MEDICI DMC
101	871	8328	213	295	8414
102	551	8748	214	294	845 ?
103	552	8027	219	256	8414
104	472	8026	222	291A	8871
105	473	8725	230	–	–
106	474	8484	231	521	8214
108	313	8324	232	152	8203
113	334	–	233	–	8203 ?
114	335	–	302	752	8151
117	767	8114	303	754	–
121	477	–	304	755	8153
124	478	–	305	704	8818
125	479	–	307	942	8816
126	208	–	308	944	–
128	186	–	330	877	Ecru
133	–	–	331	841	8515
201	542	8405	401	884	–
204	345	–	402	885	–
205	348	–	403	102	–
207	254	8411	413	603	–
208	255	8412	414	605	–
209	245	8422	419	–	8123
210	–	–	429	926	8206